365 SCIENCE EXPERIMENTS

'Science was never so much fun!'

Reprinted in 2018

 Om
KIDZ

An imprint of Om Books International

Corporate & Editorial Office
A-12, Sector 64, Noida - 201 301
Uttar Pradesh, India
Phone: +91-120-477 4100
Email: editorial@ombooks.com
Website: www.ombooksinternational.com

Sales Office
107, Ansari Road, Darya Ganj, New Delhi - 110 002, India
Phone: +91-11- 4000 9000
Fax: +91-11-2327 8091
Email: sales@ombooks.com
Website: www.ombooks.com

ISBN 978-93-83202-81-2

Printed in India

10 9 8 7 6 5 4

365 SCIENCE EXPERIMENTS

'Science was never so much fun!'

Om
KIDZ
An imprint of Om Books International

CONTENTS

MAGNETIC MAGIC
Experiments on the principle of magnetism

GETTING HOT IN HERE
Experiments on the principle of heat

ALL FALL DOWN
Experiments on the principle of gravity

RELAX – DON'T BE DENSE!
Experiments on the principle of density

LET THERE BE LIGHT
Experiments on the principle of light

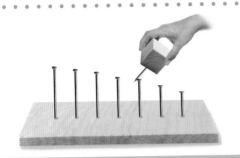

SOUND EFFECTS
Experiments on the principle of sound

UNDER PRESSURE
Experiments on the principle of air pressure

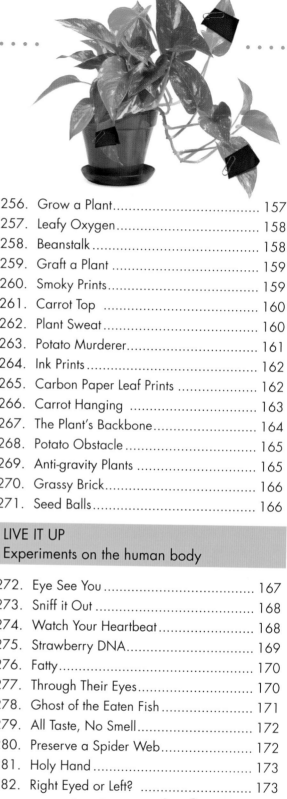

THE AIRY GODMOTHER
Experiments involving the other properties of air

GO GREEN
Experiments with plants

LIVE IT UP
Experiments on the human body

GOT YOU!
Science tricks and pranks

HIGH AND DRY
Experiments with water

SHOCKING
Experiments on the principle of static

CURRENT AFFAIRS
Experiments on the principle of electricity

ALL ELSE UNDER THE SUN
Miscellaneous experiments

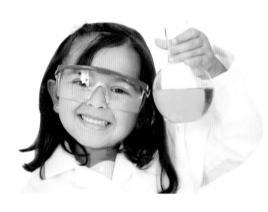

Iconic Encounters

Duration of Experiment	Difficulty Level	Adult Supervision
5 mins		
This icon indicates approximately how long the experiment will take, including the set-up time.	The black bars in this icon indicate that the experiment is most difficult.	This icon indicates that parental supervision is required. Always have an adult beside you.

NOTE: All activities and experiments described in this book should be ideally performed with adult supervision. Parents and guardians are advised to oversee the children and assist them with any difficult or potentially harmful tools. Common sense and discretion are advised. The publisher does not assume any responsibility for any injuries or damages arising from any activities.

Tsp - teaspoon   **Tbsp** - tablespoon   **ml** - millilitre   **l** - litre   **g** - gram   **1 cup** - 250 ml

KABOOM!

Experiments that involve explosive reactions

Have you ever met two people who just can't get along with each other? Chemical substances are quite the same. Sometimes they blend together perfectly well and create a third substance altogether, but occasionally, they just can't get along, and KABOOM! You have an explosion on your hands.

Let's try out some harmless chemical explosions. But remember, chemicals can be dangerous. Make sure an adult is present for all these experiments.

1. Elephant's Toothpaste

Duration of Experiment: 10 mins.   Difficulty Level:

What you need:

Dishwashing liquid

Plastic bottle

3 tbsp. warm water

¼ cup hydrogen peroxide liquid

8 drops blue food colouring

Small cup

1 tbsp. dry yeast

What to do:

Step 1. Pour the hydrogen peroxide into the bottle.

Step 2. Add the food colouring.

Step 3. Add the dishwashing liquid and mix it.

Step 4. Separately, mix the warm water and dry yeast in the cup.

Step 5. Pour this in the bottle and enjoy the foam.

What just happened? The yeast helped to remove the oxygen from the hydrogen peroxide. Since it did this very fast, it created lots and lots of bubbles.

2. Volcano in a Cup

Duration of Experiment: 20 mins.   Difficulty Level:

What you need:

Wax candle   Fireproof glass container   Cold water   Sand

What to do:

Step 1. Put some wax at the bottom of the container.

Step 2. Fill about half the container with sand.

Step 3. Fill the rest with cold water.

Step 4. Heat the container and wait a while for your waxy explosion to take place.

💡 **What just happened?** Just like in a real volcano, once the wax melted, the pressure increased. It found a weak spot in the sand and burst out from there, looking like an actual volcanic eruption.

3. Smoky Snake

Duration of Experiment: 🕐 10 mins.   Difficulty Level:

What you need:

Protective eyewear and gloves   100 ml sulphuric acid   10 g sugar   Strong glass

❗ This reaction creates a lot of heat, so be careful while handling the glass.

What to do:

Step 1. Wear protective eyewear and gloves.

Step 2. Put the sugar in the strong glass.

Step 3. Add the sulphuric acid to the glass and stir well.

Step 4. Wait for around 10 minutes and watch a smoky snake rise out of the glass!

💡 **What just happened?** The water from the sugar got sucked up by the acid and formed carbon. This carbon, along with water vapour, is what you saw as the snake.

4. Volcano Vesuvius

Duration of Experiment: 15 mins. Difficulty Level: ▬▬ ▬▬ ☰

What you need:

| 2 tsp. baking soda | ½ cup cooking vinegar | Plastic bottle | Clay | Container | 5 drops red food colouring |

What to do:

Step 1. Pat some clay around the plastic bottle in the shape of a volcano.

You can paint it brown and paint some trees on it to make it look more realistic.

Step 2. Put the baking soda in the bottle.

Step 3. Separately, pour the cooking vinegar into the container

till it is half full. Mix the food colouring with this.

Step 4. Then, pour this mixture into the bottle.

Watch as your volcano erupts in your room!

What just happened? The baking soda and cooking vinegar react to form carbonic acid, which is an unstable substance. It breaks apart into water and carbon dioxide, creating all the fizz.

SCIENCE AROUND US

Why do volcanoes erupt?

The layer just below the surface of the Earth is known as the 'mantle'. Sometimes, certain conditions cause the mantle to get heated and become liquid. When the pressure is high enough, this liquid searches for weak spots on the Earth's surface and shoots out in the form of red, hot lava.

5. Bloody Explosion

Duration of Experiment: 5 mins.   Difficulty Level:

What you need:

Ketchup   3 tbsp. baking   Water   Bottle
                    soda

What to do:

Step 1. Mix a little water and some ketchup in the bottle.

Step 2. Add the baking soda to the ketchup.

Step 3. Shut the lid of the bottle and shake it around a bit.

Step 4. Put it down and wait for the explosion.

! This experiment is quite messy, so make sure you do it in the kitchen or some place that's easy to clean up.

💡 **What just happened?** The ketchup contains acid, which reacts with the baking soda to create carbon dioxide. The gas bubbles rise up through the ketchup.

6. Bag Bomb

Duration of Experiment: 10 mins.   Difficulty Level:

What you need:

Zip lock bag   3 tsp. baking   ¼ cup warm   ½ cup cooking   Tissue paper
                     soda   water   vinegar

! Don't stand too close to the bag.

What to do:

Step 1. Pour the warm water in the zip lock bag. Add the cooking vinegar.

Step 2. Wrap the baking soda in the tissue paper.

Step 3. Close half the zip lock bag. Through the open half, put the tissue paper in the bag and close it.

Step 4. Put the bag in the sink. Step back. The bag will begin to expand, and finally burst with a bang!

💡 **What just happened?** The baking soda and cooking vinegar create a reaction, which releases carbon dioxide. The carbon dioxide fills the bag till the bag can no longer hold it and it bursts.

7. Scotch Mints and Diet Cola

Duration of Experiment: 5 mins.   Difficulty Level:

What you need:

Diet Cola   ½ Scotch Mints   Funnel

What to do:

Step 1. Find a large, open area outside your house.

Step 2. Stand the Diet Cola upright and unscrew the lid.

Step 3. Put the funnel in the neck of the bottle.

Step 4. Drop the Scotch Mints into the bottle, remove the funnel and move away immediately.

Step 5. The Diet Cola will shoot up, just like water does in a geyser.

! Make sure you do not do this indoors and stay far away from the bottle after emptying the Mentos.

What just happened? Diet Cola contains carbon dioxide, which makes it fizzy. The surface of the Scotch Mints is covered in little dimples. This means that there is a greater area for the Scotch Mints to react with the Diet Cola. Dropping the Scotch Mints in the bottle speeds up the release of the carbon dioxide, creating an explosion.

8. Flour Bomb

Duration of Experiment: 10 mins.   Difficulty Level:

What you need:

Large tin   Candle   1 tsp. flour   Funnel   Rubber pipe   Matchsticks

> **!** Make sure no one is standing close to the tin as the lid might hit them.

What to do:

Step 1. Make a hole at the bottom of the tin. Put the rubber pipe through this.

Step 2. Put the funnel on the pipe in the tin and put the flour in the funnel.

Step 3. Light the candle using a matchstick put it at the bottom of the tin and close its lid.

Step 4. Quickly blow into the rubber tube and see the lid of the tin fly off with a bang.

> **What just happened?** The candle heats the air, causing it to expand. When you blow into the tin, the flour catches fire for a split second. This increases the pressure and causes the tin to pop.

9. Sparkly Explosion

Duration of Experiment: 10 mins.   Difficulty Level:

What you need:

Vase   2 tbsp. baking soda   ½ cup cooking vinegar   Tray   2 tsp. blue glitter   5 drops red food colouring

What to do:

Step 1. Put the baking soda in the vase.

Step 2. Place this vase in the tray.

Step 3. Add the food colouring and glitter.

Step 4. Pour in the cooking vinegar quickly.

Step 5. Enjoy your shiny display.

> **What just happened?** The baking soda and cooking vinegar react to form carbonic acid, which is an unstable substance. It breaks apart into water and carbon dioxide, creating all the fizz.

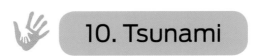

10. Tsunami

Duration of Experiment: ⏱ 10 mins.   Difficulty Level: ▬ ▬▬ ▬▬

What you need:

| 35 mm film canister | Clay | 1 Antacid tablet | Bucket | Water |

What to do:

Step 1. Fill the bucket with water.

Step 2. Coat the canister with the clay so that it looks like a volcano. It should also be heavy enough to keep the canister from floating.

Step 3. Fill $\frac{1}{3}^{rd}$ of the canister with water.

Step 4. Break the Antacid tablet and drop one quarter into the canister.

Step 5. Close the canister and stick it at the bottom of the bucket which is filled with water.

Step 6. After a minute, the canister lid will fly off, causing a tsunami-like wave.

💡 **What just happened?** The reaction in the canister produces carbon dioxide. The carbon dioxide increases the pressure, till the force is enough to force open the lid of the canister. The disturbance underwater pushes a relatively large volume of water to the surface, creating a model tsunami.

11. Bag Blast

Duration of Experiment: 10 mins.   Difficulty Level: ▬▬ ▬▬ ▬▬

What you need:

6 lemons   1 tsp. baking soda   50ml Water   Zip lock bag

Don't stand too close to the bag.

What to do:

Step 1. Squeeze the lemons into the zip lock bag.

Step 2. Add baking soda with the spoon.

Step 3. Quickly add water and shut it.

Step 4. Put it in the sink and leave it.

Step 5. The bag becomes extremely cold and blows up!

What just happened? Lemon contains citric acid. This acid reacts with the water and baking soda. The reaction creates carbon dioxide, which fills the bag and causes it to blow up.

12. Hot Ice

Duration of Experiment: 2 hours   Difficulty Level: ▬▬ ▬▬ ▬▬

What you need:

Saucepan   1 l clear vinegar   4 tbsp. baking soda   Water

What to do:

Step 1. Empty the vinegar and baking soda in the saucepan a little at a time, stirring regularly.

Step 2. Boil the solution for about an hour until you see a thin layer form on the surface.

Step 3. Remove it from the heat and cover it immediately. Make sure there are no crystals. If there are, add some water and vinegar to dissolve them.

Step 4. Place it in the freezer to chill.

Step 5. When you remove it, it will still be in a liquid form. Touch it to see it solidify instantly and give off heat!

What just happened? Sodium acetate (the substance you created), or 'hot ice', remains liquid even below its melting point. Touching the solution triggers the crystallisation process, releasing heat in the process.

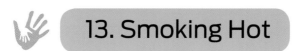

13. Smoking Hot

Duration of Experiment: ⏱ 1 hour   Difficulty Level: ▬▬ ▬▬ ▬

What you need:

1 cup sugar   3 cups potassium nitrate   Pan   Aluminium foil   5 cm string   Lighter   Naphtha lighter fluid

What to do:

Step 1. Dip the string in lighter fluid. Let it dry.

Step 2. Pour potassium nitrate and sugar into the pan. Heat on a low flame.

Step 3. Use long strokes to stir the mixture till it is nearly liquid.

Step 4. Once it is brown, take it off the heat.

Step 5. Empty it into an aluminium foil. This is now your smoke bomb.

Step 6. Put the dry string in the smoke bomb.

Step 7. Allow the bomb to cool and peel off the aluminium foil. Light it and stand back.

⚠ Perform this experiment only in an open area and under strict adult supervision.

💡 **What just happened?** When heated, the sugar and potassium nitrate react and form a substance called potassium carbonate. When this solid is dispersed into the air it blocks light, giving the 'smoky' effect.

14. Bottled Cannon

Duration of Experiment: ⏱ 10 mins.   Difficulty Level:

What you need:

Wine bottle   Cork   4 tbsp. cooking vinegar   1 tsp. baking soda   Tissue paper   2 pencils

What to do:

Step 1. Put the cooking vinegar in the bottle. It should not spill over when the bottle is laid on its side.

Step 2. Wrap the baking soda in the tissue paper. Put it in the bottle.

Step 3. Quickly cork the bottle.

Step 4. Lay the bottle across two horizontal pencils.

Step 5. Wait for the cork to fly off!

> ❗ Make sure no one is in the path of the cork.

💡 **What just happened?** The pressure produced by the generated carbon dioxide caused the cork to be blown out and the bottle to recoil.

15. Tea Bag Rocket

Duration of Experiment: ⏱ 5 mins.   Difficulty Level:

What you need:

Tea bag   Lighter   Metal tray   Scissors

> ❗ Make sure you aren't anywhere near curtains or anything flammable. Try to perform this outdoors if possible.

What to do:

Step 1. Cut the top of the tea bag.

Step 2. Pour the tea leaves out.

Step 3. Open the bag so that it forms a cylinder.

Step 4. Place it on the tray.

Step 5. Use the lighter to light the top of the tea bag.

💡 **What just happened?** Lighting the tea bag caused the air inside to heat up. We all know that hot air rises. The tea bag was light enough for the air to lift along with it.

REACTIONARY

Experiments that involve chemical reactions

Unlike the angry substances in the previous section, most substances are rather docile and get along with each other just fine. In this section, you will encounter several chemicals that react with each other to form another substance.

Though most of the experiments are less volatile than those in the previous section, remember that fire can be dangerous. Always have an adult around whenever you are trying to perform any experiment that includes fire.

16. Jumping Spaghetti

Duration of Experiment: ⏱ **20** mins.   Difficulty Level:

What you need:

Uncooked spaghetti	Water	2 tbsp. baking soda	1 cup cooking vinegar	Glass

What to do:

Step 1. Dissolve the baking soda in the glass of water. Add cooking vinegar.

Step 2. Break the spaghetti into one-inch pieces. Put six of these in the glass.

Step 3. Watch your spaghetti jump up and down in the glass.

💡 **What just happened?** The reaction between vinegar and baking soda created carbon dioxide gas. This gas sticks to the spaghetti and makes it float on water. Hence, it rises up. On reaching the surface, the gas is released into the air and the spaghetti sinks down again.

17. Dancing Mothballs

Duration of Experiment: ⏱ 15 mins.   Difficulty Level: ▬ ▬ ▬

What you need:

| 4 mothballs | Water | 2 tsp. baking soda | ½ cup cooking vinegar | Glass |

What to do:

Step 1. Dissolve the baking soda in a glass of water.

Step 2. Add the cooking vinegar.

Step 3. Put the mothballs in the glass.

Step 4. Watch the mothballs rise to the surface and sink down again.

💡 **What just happened?** The reaction between cooking vinegar and baking soda created carbon dioxide gas. This gas stuck to the mothballs and made them float on the water. The gas was released into the air, and the mothballs sank down again.

18. Ready to Launch

Duration of Experiment: ⏱ 5 mins.   Difficulty Level: ▬ ▬ ▬

What you need:

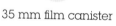

| 35 mm film canister | 1 Antacid tablet | 3 tbsp. water | Tray |

⚠ Stay far away from the rocket.

What to do:

Step 1. Find a large, open space.

Step 2. Remove the lid of the canister and put the water in it.

Step 3. Quickly put the tablet in the canister and seal it tight with the lid.

Step 4. Immediately put the canister down, with the lid on the tray.

Step 5. After about 10 seconds, the film canister will launch into the air.

💡 **What just happened?** The water and Antacid reacted to form carbon dioxide. This increased the pressure in the canister. The pressure built up till the rocket blasted. This system of thrust is how a real rocket works, whether it is in outer space or here in the Earth's atmosphere.

19. Chemical Ice cream

Duration of Experiment: **30** mins.   Difficulty Level:

What you need:

Small zip lock bag

Large zip lock bag

½ cup milk

½ cup whipping cream

¼ cup sugar

¼ tsp. vanilla flavouring

¾ cup rock salt

2 cups of ice cubes

Styrofoam cups

Gloves

> **!** Do not touch the bag without gloves as the temperature drops enough to cause tissue damage.

What to do:

Step 1. Put the sugar, milk, whipping cream and vanilla in the smaller zip lock bag. Mix it.

Step 2. Put ice in the large zip lock bag.

Step 3. Add rock salt to the ice.

Step 4. Place the smaller bag into the larger one and shut it securely.

Step 5. Using the safety gloves, hold the large bag from the top and shake the bag from side to side.

Step 6. Shake the bag for around 15 minutes.

Step 7. Remove the frozen contents of the small bag into the styrofoam cups and eat your chemical ice cream.

What just happened? Adding salt to the ice lowered the freezing point of ice. In order to reach this temperature, heat needed to be taken out from the water.

20. Create Oxygen

Duration of Experiment: **20** mins.   Difficulty Level:

What you need:

| 100 ml hydrogen peroxide (3%) | 2 tbsp. yeast | Small glass jar with lid | Toothpicks | Burning candle |

What to do:

Step 1. Pour the hydrogen peroxide into the jar.

Step 2. Add the yeast to the jar. Cover it.

Step 3. Once bubbles begin to form, light a toothpick and extinguish it.

Step 4. While the toothpick is still glowing, remove the lid and insert the toothpick in the neck of the jar.

Step 5. Your flame will be revived.

> Always be careful when handling fire. Never use fire in the absence of an adult.

> 💡 **What just happened?** The reaction between the yeast and the hydrogen peroxide created oxygen. Fire needs oxygen to burn. So, when you put the smouldering toothpick into the jar, the oxygen revived the flame.

21. Green Coins

Duration of Experiment:  **24** hours   Difficulty Level:

What you need:

| Tissue paper | Plate | 1 tbsp. salt | 3 tbsp. cooking vinegar | Copper coins | Bowl |

What to do:

Step 1. Fold the tissue paper so that it is thick.

Step 2. Mix the salt and cooking vinegar in the bowl. Soak the tissue in this mixture.

Step 3. Lay the tissue on the plate.

Step 4. Wrap the coins in the tissue.

Step 5. Check the coins the next day. They should have turned green!

> 💡 **What just happened?** The copper reacts with carbon dioxide in the air to form copper carbonate, which is green in colour. This reaction usually takes a long time to take place. The cooking vinegar and salt speeds up this reaction.

22. Kitchen Indication

Duration of Experiment: 25 mins.   Difficulty Level:

What you need:

½ red cabbage   Container   Water   Sieve   1 tbsp. baking soda   Knife   Glass

What to do:

Step 1. Chop the red cabbage and boil it in water on the stove.

Step 2. Stir well and leave it to soak for about 15 minutes.

Step 3. Once cool, strain the now purple cabbage water and discard the cabbage.

Step 4. Put the cabbage water in the container. Add the baking soda.

Step 5. Notice the colour change.

What just happened? A chemical in the red cabbage reacts with the baking soda and turns green.

23. Chemical Garden

Duration of Experiment: 2 hours   Difficulty Level:

What you need:

Jam jar   Water   Water glass   Metal salt crystals

> Be careful that the crystals don't break when you pour out the water glass.

What to do:

Step 1. Fill $\frac{1}{3}^{rd}$ of the jar with water glass.

Step 2. Fill the rest with water.

Step 3. Drop in some metal salt crystals (such as copper sulphate, lead nitrate, aluminium sulphate, ferrous chloride, etc.).

Step 4. Place your jar on a still surface.

Step 5. In a few hours, you will see your crystals 'growing'.

Step 6. Once you are happy with your garden, replace the solution with water.

What just happened? The metal salts react with the water glass to form the beautiful coloured precipitant.

24. Bubbly Colours

Duration of Experiment: 10 mins.   Difficulty Level:

What you need:

4 tsp. baking soda   2 tbsp. cooking vinegar   Food colouring   Paint palette

What to do:

Step 1. Fill four sections of the palette with cooking vinegar.

Step 2. Put a drop of each colour into the different sections.

Step 3. Put a teaspoon of baking soda into each section.

Step 4. Watch your fizzing colours!

What just happened? The cooking vinegar and baking soda react to form carbon dioxide, which causes all the fizzy bubbles.

25. Potato Starch

Duration of Experiment: 10 mins.   Difficulty Level:

What you need:

Iodine solution   Plate   Water   Potato

What to do:

Step 1. Boil and mash the potato.

Step 2. Put this on a plate and put two drops of iodine on the potato.

Step 3. Watch the iodine solution change from a brown to a purple blue colour.

What just happened? Potato contains a certain chemical called 'starch'. When this starch is in the presence of iodine, it turns blue.

26. Coloured Chemicals

Duration of Experiment: ⏱ **25** mins.   Difficulty Level: ▬ ▬ ▬

What you need:

½ red cabbage   Water   Sieve   2 tbsp. baking soda   2 lemons   Bowls   Knife

What to do:

Step 1. Chop the red cabbage and bring it to a boil on the stove.

Step 2. Let it soak for 15 minutes. Stir it occasionally.

Step 3. Once cool, strain the water and discard the cabbage.

Step 4. Squeeze the lemons and mix the juice with the cabbage water in one bowl.

Step 5. Mix baking soda with cabbage water in another bowl.

Step 6. Now mix these two solutions in a third bowl.

Step 7. Watch as the pink and green solutions mix and turn purple!

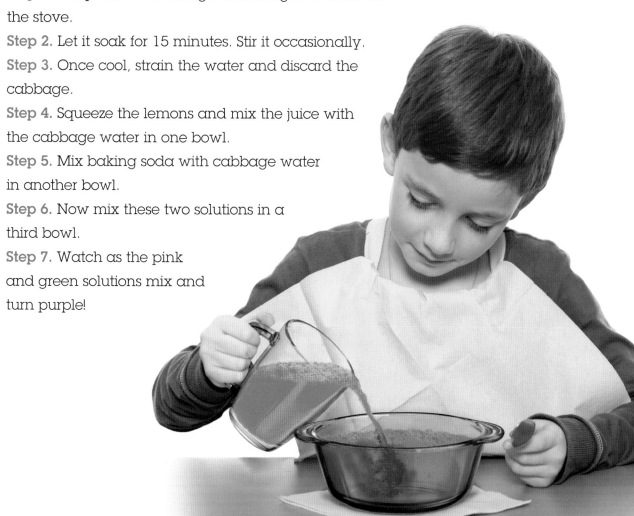

💡 **What just happened?** When citric acid and baking soda are mixed, they cancel out, or neutralise, the reactions that took place. The pink solution and green solution mix to form a third purple solution.

27. Acidic

Duration of Experiment: ⏱ **20 mins.**   Difficulty Level:

What you need:

½ red cabbage   Water   Sieve   1 lemon   Container   Knife

What to do:

Step 1. Chop the red cabbage and bring it to boil on the stove.

Step 2. Stir well and leave it to soak for about 15 minutes.

Step 3. Once cool, drain the water and throw the cabbage away.

Step 4. Put the cabbage water in the container. Squeeze the lemon.

Step 5. Notice the colour change.

💡 **What just happened?** A chemical in the red cabbage reacts with the citric acid in the lemon and turns pink.

28. Speedy Rust

Duration of Experiment: ⏱ **2 hours**   Difficulty Level:

What you need:

Steel wool   Glass   Water   3 tbsp. cooking vinegar   3 tbsp. bleach   Gloves

What to do:

Step 1. Put the steel wool in the glass.

Step 2. Fill the glass with water.

Step 3. Pour in the cooking vinegar and bleach.

Step 4. Wait for two hours and see your steel wool pad rust!

❗ Be careful while handling the bleach. Use latex gloves.

💡 **What just happened?** Rust forms when iron is combined with moisture and oxygen. The oxygen in the bleach combines with the iron in the wool to form rust.

29. Rusty

Duration of Experiment: ⏱ **48** hours   Difficulty Level: ▬ ▬ ▬

What you need:

Test tube   Water   2 tsp. cooking vinegar   Container   Steel wool

What to do:

Step 1. Dip the steel wool in a mixture of vinegar and water.

Step 2. Put some steel wool in the test tube.

Step 3. Fill the container with water.

Step 4. Invert the test tube and place it in the container.

Step 5. Leave your apparatus untouched for two days.

You will see the steel wool rust and the water level in the test tube rise.

SCIENCE AROUND US

Why do objects rust?

Rust is the common name for a compound called iron oxide (Fe_2O_3). Iron (Fe) combines with oxygen from the air very easily. Actually, iron reacts with oxygen so easily that pure iron is rarely found in nature. When iron (or steel) reacts with oxygen, it forms the red coloured substance called iron oxide.

💡 **What just happened?** The vinegar helped speed up the process of rusting. This used up oxygen. As the oxygen in the air was being used up, the air pressure decreased and the water was sucked into the tube.

ICKY, GOOEY, SQUISHY

Experiments that are every parent's nightmare

By the end of this section, you will have made all sorts of icky things like fake snot, fake puke and fake slime. You will also have your very own mouldy orange. But try not to make too much of a mess while making these things, or you may also end up being grounded for two weeks!

Go on... get started... if you dare...

30. Crazy Putty

Duration of Experiment: ⏱ 12 mins.   Difficulty Level: ▬ ■ ■

What you need:

Container   Water   Glue   1 tbsp. borax   Spoon

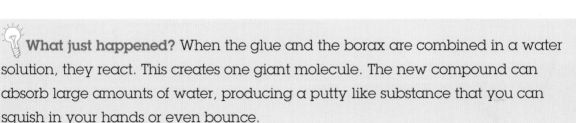

What to do:

Step 1. Fill the bottom of the container with glue.

Step 2. Add the same amount of water and stir.

Step 3. Add borax. Stir the mixture.

Step 4. It will soon join together, acting like putty!

💡 **What just happened?** When the glue and the borax are combined in a water solution, they react. This creates one giant molecule. The new compound can absorb large amounts of water, producing a putty like substance that you can squish in your hands or even bounce.

31. Quicksand

Duration of Experiment: **20** mins.   Difficulty Level:

What you need:

1 cup cornflour

Large container

Wooden spoon

½ cup water

What to do:

Step 1. Place the cornflour in the container and slowly add water to it, stirring continuously.

Step 2. Stir till it gets the consistency of honey.

Step 3. Stir it around slowly and it will feel like liquid. But if you try to stir it quickly, it will turn solid.

Step 4. Try dropping something in this mixture, when it is solid and watch how it slowly gets swallowed up!

SCIENCE AROUND US

Quicksand

Real quicksand works in a similar manner to the quicksand you just made. When normal sand becomes so saturated with water that the friction between the sand is reduced, it becomes quicksand. If you ever get stuck in quicksand, just relax. Your body will soon float up.

What just happened? When the thick mixture was stirred quickly, it became solid. The cornflour grains can't slide over each other due to a lack of water between them. When you stirred slowly, you allowed more water between the cornflour grains, letting them slide over each other more easily.

32. Make Fake Snot

Duration of Experiment: 5 mins.   Difficulty Level: ▬ ▬ ▬

What you need:

Fork   Cup   Boiling water   Gelatine   ¼ cup corn syrup   Green food colouring

What to do:

Step 1. Fill half a cup with boiling water.

Step 2. Add three teaspoons of gelatine powder to it. Let it soften before stirring with a fork.

Step 3. Add the corn syrup and green food colouring.

Step 4. Stir it again. It looks like snot, doesn't it?

What just happened? Mucus is made mostly of sugars and protein. This is exactly what you used to make the fake snot. The long, fine strings you see inside the fake snot when you moved it around are protein strands.

33. Make Slime

Duration of Experiment: 5 mins.   Difficulty Level: ▬ ▬ ▬

What you need:

Bowl   ¼ cup glue   ¼ cup liquid starch   6 drops food colouring   ¼ cup water   Spoon

What to do:

Step 1. Pour all the water into the bowl.

Step 2. Add the glue and mix well.

Step 3. Add food colouring to the mixture.

Step 4. Now add the liquid starch and stir it in.

Step 5. You just made fake slime!

What just happened? Glue is made up of tiny strands. The liquid starch helps these strands to stay together, giving it a slimy feel.

34. Paper Mache Pots

Duration of Experiment: ⏱ 48 hours   Difficulty Level: ▬ ▬▬ ▬▬

What you need:

Newspaper

Large container

Sieve

Potato masher

Hot water

Yoghurt cup

What to do:

Step 1. Tear the newspaper into very small pieces and soak them in the container in hot water overnight.

Step 2. Drain out the excess water and mash the paper using a potato masher.

Step 3. Once it achieves a pulpy, liquid consistency, fill it in the yoghurt cup.

Step 4. Remove it from the cup and pour it into a sieve. Drain out the excess water.

Step 5. Coat the sides of the yoghurt cup with the drained pulp and put it on a window sill to dry.

Step 6. Remove it from the cup after two days.

Step 7. Paint it to look pretty. You can now grow your own plant in the pot!

💡 **What just happened?** The water is absorbed by the pulp, making it easier to reshape. The pulp pots maintain their new shape even after drying.

35. Milk Plastic!

Duration of Experiment: 2 days   Difficulty Level:

What you need:

1 tbsp. cooking vinegar | Strainer | Warm milk | Cutters | Cup

What to do:

Step 1. Put a tablespoon of cooking vinegar in a cup of warm milk and stir it well.

Step 2. Pour the milk through the strainer. You should be left with a white lumpy solid.

Step 3. Wait for it to cool. Press it into any shape you like and let it dry for a couple of days.

Don't try to drink the milk or eat the plastic!

What just happened? You made a protein called 'casein'. This protein in the milk reacted with the acid in the vinegar and formed lumps, which were easy to mould.

36. Mould it

Duration of Experiment: 2 weeks   Difficulty Level:

What you need:

Oranges | Cotton balls | Zip lock bag | Rubber gloves

Handle the mouldy oranges with gloves. Don't eat or smell the mould.

What to do:

Step 1. Leave the oranges in the open for a day.

Step 2. Place them with a damp cotton ball in the zip lock bag.

Step 3. Seal it and put it in a warm, damp place.

Step 4. Check the bag after two weeks.

Step 5. You will see little fuzzy balls on the oranges.

What just happened? The little fuzzy balls are called 'mould'. It is a form of fungus that grows faster in warm, moist places.

37. Bread Spores

Duration of Experiment: 🕐 **2 days**   Difficulty Level: ▬ ▬ ▬

What you need:

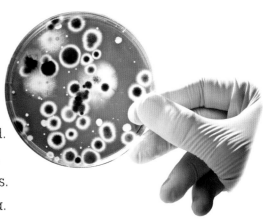

Bread   Zip lock bag   Milk carton   5 drops water   Rubber gloves

Be careful while handling the mould and don't smell it.

What to do:

Step 1. Put water on the bread.

Step 2. Seal the bread in the zip lock bag and put it in the milk carton. Wear rubber gloves while handling the bread.

Step 3. Open it after two days to see mould spores of various colours and textures.

💡 **What just happened?** Spores develop into living fungus when the conditions are suitable, such as on the damp bread.

38. Grow Bacteria

Duration of Experiment: 🕐 **3 days**   Difficulty Level: ▬ ▬ ▬

What you need:

Petri dish   Gelatine   Ear buds   Newspaper

What to do:

Step 1. Make a gelatine solution in the petri dish. Let it solidify.

Step 2. Collect dust from your house on the ear bud.

Step 3. Rub it on the petri dish and put the lid on it.

Step 4. Keep the dish in a warm area for three days.

Step 5. Check the dish to see the growth of bacteria.

Step 6. Dispose the dish by wrapping it in newspaper and throwing it in the bin.

💡 **What just happened?** Soft, moist and warm conditions are ideal for the growth of bacteria.

39. Dancing Goop

Duration of Experiment: 15 mins. Difficulty Level:

What you need:

| Speaker | 2 cups cornstarch | Thin metal cookie sheet | Paint | Water |

What to do:

Step 1. Mix water with cornstarch until it achieves the consistency of honey.

Step 2. Spread this mixture on the cookie sheet.

Step 3. Add different coloured paint to the mixture.

Step 4. Place the sheet on a speaker and play loud music.

Step 5. Hold the edges of the sheet and watch your goop dance!

What just happened? Sound is caused by vibrations. The special texture of the goop made it dance in the presence of these vibrations.

40. Sticky

Duration of Experiment: 15 mins. Difficulty Level:

What you need:

| 1 cup flour | ½ cup water | Jar | Spoon | Newspaper | Brush |

What to do:

Step 1. Mix the flour and water in the jar.

Step 2. Stir the mixture well for five minutes.

Step 3. Spread the glue on the newspaper with the brush and let it dry for 15 minutes.

What just happened? A chemical reaction took place once the flour was mixed with the water. The water evaporated and the flour held the paper together.

41. Homemade Gloop

Duration of Experiment: 20 mins.   Difficulty Level:

What you need:

1 tsp. borax   1 tbsp. glue   Cup   Bowl   6 tbsps. water   Spoon

What to do:

Step 1. Mix the borax and five tablespoons of the water in the bowl. Stir till it dissolves.

Step 2. Mix glue and the remaining water separately in the cup.

Step 3. Put two teaspoons of the borax-water mixture from the container in the cup. Stir it.

Step 4. Once it turns into a lump, take it out and knead it in your hand for two minutes.

Step 5. Have fun playing with your gloop.

What just happened? The borax holds together the molecules in the glue, making it more solid. When tense, the gloop acts like a solid. But when relaxed, the gloop acts like a liquid.

42. Glowing Goo

Duration of Experiment: 5 mins.   Difficulty Level:

What you need:

1 tsp. borax   ½ cup glue   1½ cup warm water   ½ tbsp. glow in the dark paint   Bowl and Whisk

What to do:

Step 1. Mix the borax with 1 cup of warm water.

Step 2. Add the paint to this mixture.

Step 3. Separately whisk the glue and the remaining water with a whisk.

Step 4. Mix both solutions with your hand.

Step 5. Drain out the extra water. Enjoy the glowing goo.

What just happened? When the glue and the borax are combined in a water solution, they react and create one giant molecule that can absorb large amounts of water. This glows in the dark when you mix the paint with it.

43. Make a Bouncy Ball

Duration of Experiment: 30 mins.   Difficulty Level: ▬ ▬▬ ▬▬▬

What you need:

½ tsp. borax | 1 tbsp. cornstarch | 1 tbsp. glue | 2 tbsps. warm water | Food colouring | Spoon | Plastic containers

What to do:

Step 1. Pour the water and borax in one container.

Step 2. Add food colouring. Stir the mixture with a spoon till the borax dissolves.

Step 3. Separately, pour glue, half a teaspoon of the borax solution you just made and cornstarch.

Step 4. Leave the mixture alone for 15 seconds and stir it again till it becomes too thick to stir any more.

Step 5. Take it out of the container. Mould it in the shape of a ball with your hands till it becomes solid. You can bounce it and play with it if you wish.

What just happened? The reaction between the borax and the glue helps create chains of molecules that stay together when you pick them up.

The cornstarch binds the molecules together so that they maintain their shape.

44. Fake Puke

Duration of Experiment: 15 mins.   Difficulty Level:

What you need:

Applesauce   Raisin   Oatmeal   1 pack gelatine   Pan   Spoon   Tray

What to do:

Step 1. Mix the gelatine and applesauce in a pan on a low flame till it is completely dissolved.

Step 2. Add some oatmeal and raisin, and stir it.

Step 3. Take it off the heat.

Step 4. Spread it out on the tray and let it cool.

Step 5. You can eat it – if you dare.

💡 **What just happened?** Heating the applesauce made it thinner than when it was cool. The oatmeal and raisin give it the lumpy texture that is often found in puke.

45. Green Ball

Duration of Experiment: 30 mins.   Difficulty Level:

What you need:

1 tbsp. borax   1 cup water   Glue   Green food colouring   Zip lock bag   Styrofoam beads

What to do:

Step 1. Mix borax in half a cup of water.

Step 2. Mix glue and $\frac{1}{4}^{th}$ cup water. Add the food colouring.

Step 3. Pour both solutions into the zip lock bag. Don't mix it.

Step 4. Add the styrofoam beads.

Step 5. Seal the bag and knead it with your hand till it is mixed.

Step 6. Take it out and shape it as you wish.

💡 **What just happened?** When the glue and the borax are combined in a water solution, they create one giant molecule. The styrofoam beads help keep the shape.

WHAT'S COOKING?

Experiments with kitchen materials

Do you know that many items from your kitchen can actually be used as substitute chemicals in science experiments? There is science in just about everything around us.

I bet you didn't know that you could actually make an electric battery using a lemon. In this section, you can find out how.

Just make sure you tell your parents when you finish all the vinegar in the house, unless you want to run an errand and buy more!

46. Hot Soap

Duration of Experiment: 5 mins.   Difficulty Level: ▬ ▬ ▬

What you need:

Soap bar   Microwave   Flat microwave dish

What to do:

Step 1. Put the soap on the microwave dish.

Step 2. Microwave it for two minutes.

Step 3. Watch the phenomenal growth of your soap!

Don't leave the microwave and soap unattended.

💡 **What just happened?** When you heat the soap, you not only soften it, but also heat the air and water trapped inside it. The water vaporises and the air expands. The expanding gases push on the soft soap, creating the foam.

47. Hot Ice cream

Duration of Experiment: ⏱ 1 hour   Difficulty Level: ▬ ▬ ■

What you need:

| 3 eggs | ¼ tsp. cream of tartar | ¼ tsp. salt | ½ tsp. vanilla essence | 1 cup sugar | Ice cream | Cookies |

Baking tray   Egg whisk   Bowl   Oven

What to do:

Step 1. Separate the egg whites from the yolks in the bowl.

Step 2. Add the cream of tartar, salt and vanilla essence to the egg whites.

Step 3. Whip the whites till they are nice and fluffy.

Step 4. Add sugar by sprinkling one tablespoon at a time over the mixture.

Step 5. Keep stirring the mixture.

Step 6. Put the cookies in the baking tray at an equal distance from each other.

Step 7. Now put a small scoop of ice cream on each of the cookies.

Step 8. Coat the ice cream with the mixture you just prepared.

Step 9. Bake your ice cream cookie in an oven at 110°C.

Step 10. Take it out after an hour and enjoy your piping hot ice cream!

💡 **What just happened?** Cream of tartar is acidic. When it turns moist, it releases carbon dioxide. There are air pockets in the whipped egg, too. The sugar in the mixture hardens when heated and traps the air in the mixture. Air is a poor conductor of heat and therefore protects the ice cream from the heat of the oven.

48. Gelatine Mobile

Duration of Experiment: **48** hours   Difficulty Level:

What you need:

3 small packets gelatine	Cookie cutters	Food colouring	Plastic lid	Saucepan	5 tbsp. water

Wooden spoon   Straw

What to do:

Step 1. Cook water, food colouring and gelatine in a saucepan on a low heat on the stove till it is thick.

Step 2. Pour the liquid into the plastic lid and remove the bubbles with the spoon.

Step 3. Let the mixture cool for 45 minutes.

Step 4. Carefully take the gelatine out of the plastic lid.

Step 5. While the gelatine is still elastic, use the cookie cutters to cut out various shapes.

Step 6. Use the straw to make holes in the shapes, so they can be hung.

Step 7. Leave them out to dry for a couple of days and they'll be as hard as plastic!

What just happened? Gelatine dissolves in water only when heated, but not when it is cool. So when the gelatine solution cooled down, it formed a semi-solid mass or gel.

49. Colour Symphony

Duration of Experiment: ⏱ **5** mins.   Difficulty Level: ▬ ▬▬ ▬▬

What you need:

Food colouring   Tray   Whole milk   5 drops dish-washing soap

What to do:

Step 1. Pour a thin layer of milk onto the tray.

Step 2. Add six drops of different coloured food colouring onto the milk in different spots.

Step 3. Add the dishwashing soap onto the drops of food colouring.

Step 4. Watch the colours go berserk.

💡 **What just happened?** Soap breaks down fat. The liquid soap onto the tray tried to break down the fat in the milk. While it was doing that, it caused the colours to scatter.

50. Colour Changing Juice

Duration of Experiment: ⏱ **10** mins.   Difficulty Level: ▬ ▬▬ ▬▬

What you need:

Grape juice   5 lemons   2 tsp. baking soda   Glasses

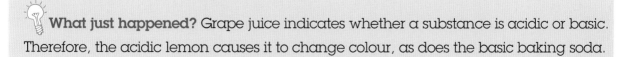

What to do:

Step 1. Empty the grape juice into one glass.

Step 2. Squeeze the lemons into this glass.
Notice the colour change from purple to pink!

Step 3. In the other glass, mix some grape juice and baking soda.
Watch the colour change from purple to green!

💡 **What just happened?** Grape juice indicates whether a substance is acidic or basic. Therefore, the acidic lemon causes it to change colour, as does the basic baking soda.

51. Silver Eggs

Duration of Experiment: ⏱ **10** mins. Difficulty Level:

What you need:

Raw egg   Candle   Water   Tong

What to do:

Step 1. Blacken the egg by holding it with tongs over a flame.

Step 2. Put it in the jar of water.

Step 3. See the soot disappear and watch it start to shine.

💡 **What just happened?** The carbon in the soot repels the water and holds a thin film of air in the egg's surface. This layer of air under the soot gives the egg a silvery coat.

52. Starchy

Duration of Experiment: ⏱ **4** hours Difficulty Level:

What you need:

Potato   Handkerchief   Water   Bowl   Knife

What to do:

Step 1. Cut the potato into small pieces. Wrap them in the handkerchief.

Step 2. Dip the handkerchief with the potatoes in a bowl filled with water.

Step 3. Take them out and squeeze the handkerchief.

Step 4. Continue to dip and squeeze until the water changes colour.

Step 5. Leave the bowl alone in a sunny area for a few hours.

Step 6. This substance left behind in the bowl is called starch.

💡 **What just happened?** Foods like potatoes contain a large amount of starch. This is used by our body as a source of quick energy.

53. Squishy Egg

Duration of Experiment: ⏱ **7 days**   Difficulty Level: ▬ ▬ ▬

What you need:

Raw egg

Large bowl

Cooking vinegar

What to do:

Step 1. Put the egg into a bowl and cover it completely with vinegar.

Step 2. Wait for a week and drain the vinegar.

Step 3. You can now play with your rubber egg!

Step 4. Be careful though, don't break the membrane!

💡 **What just happened?** Vinegar, an acid, dissolves the calcium in the eggshell. Calcium makes the shell hard. But a thin, flexible membrane just under the shell still holds the egg's shape.

54. Egg Bubbles

Duration of Experiment: ⏱ **10 mins.**   Difficulty Level: ▬ ▬ ▬

What you need:

Jar

Hot water

Raw egg

What to do:

Step 1. Place the egg carefully into the glass or jar.

Step 2. Carefully add hot water until it is nearly full.

Step 3. Leave it on a table or a flat surface.

Step 4. See tiny bubbles rise to the surface.

💡 **What just happened?** An egg contains a small air pocket at its larger end between the shell and egg white. When the air trapped inside this small pocket begins to heat up, it expands and tries to find a way out of the shell.

55. Air Freshener

Duration of Experiment: 2 hours   Difficulty Level:

What you need:

| 4 packets gelatine | Water | 15 drops fragrance oil | Food colouring | Small jars | 1 tbsp. salt |

What to do:

Step 1. Boil one cup of water. Dissolve the gelatine in it.

Step 2. Take it off the heat and add a cup of cold water.

Step 3. Add the fragrance oil, food colouring and salt.

Step 4. Pour this mixture into the small jars. Refrigerate for 2 hours.

Step 5. Place these around your house to smell the fragrance.

> ! **Always take an adult's assistance when you are using the stove.**

What just happened? Gelatine is a polymer. To hold its shape, it has a matrix-like structure which is like a matrix. The particles of fragrance oil are suspended in this structure. The scent particles are released as the gel evaporates.

56. Fishing Ice

Duration of Experiment: 15 mins.   Difficulty Level:

What you need:

| Ice cubes | String | Salt | Glass |

What to do:

Step 1. Put an ice cube in a glass.

Step 2. Dangle the string and hold it still over the ice cube.

Step 3. Sprinkle some salt on it.

Step 4. Wait for two minutes and lift your ice cube with the string.

What just happened? Salt lowers the freezing point of water. The salt begins to crystallise and ice refreezes around the string. This makes the ice cube stick to the string.

57. Fruit Battery

Duration of Experiment: ⏱ 15 mins.   Difficulty Level: ▬▬ ▬▬ ▬▬

What you need:

Lime   Copper nail   Small light bulb   Electric tape   Wire

What to do:

Step 1. Squeeze the lime without breaking its skin.

Step 2. Insert both nails into the fruit at a distance of two inches from each other.

Step 3. Peel the plastic insulation off the bulb (leads of the light).

Step 4. Wrap the wires around the head of the two nails.

Step 5. Secure the wire around the nails using electric tape.

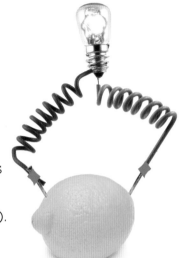

💡 **What just happened?** Citric fruits conduct electricity because of their acidic content. The different charges of the lime and the nail causes the electric flow.

58. Salty Ice Experiment

Duration of Experiment: ⏱ 30 mins.   Difficulty Level: ▬▬ ▬▬ ▬▬

What you need:

Glasses   Salt   Water

What to do:

Step 1. Fill half the glasses with water.

Step 2. Add salt to one of the glasses and stir it.

Step 3. Put both glasses in the fridge at the same time.

Step 4. Check your glasses every 10 minutes to see which one freezes first.

Step 5. You will notice that the salty water remains liquid longer than the plain water!

💡 **What just happened?** Adding salt to water lowers the freezing point. This means that it takes longer for salty water to freeze at the same temperature than normal water.

59. Floating Eggs

Duration of Experiment: ⏱ **10** mins.   Difficulty Level: ▬▬ ▬▬ ▬▬

What you need:

Raw eggs   6 tbsps. salt   Water   2 glasses

What to do:

Step 1. Add the salt to half a glass of water.

Step 2. Pour tap water till the glass is full. Try not to mix the salt water and plain water.

Step 3. Fill the other glass with tap water.

Step 4. Gently lower the eggs into both the glasses. It will not sink all the way to the bottom in the salty glass. Instead, it will float in the middle of the glass with the salty water.

SCIENCE AROUND US

Salty Seas

It is easier to float in the sea than in a swimming pool because of its salt content. In fact, the salt content in the Dead Sea is so high that it is almost impossible to drown!

💡 **What just happened?** The denser salt water remains at the bottom of the glass. It is easy for the egg to float in salt water but not in tap water. The egg sinks through the tap water till it reaches the salt water and floats.

60. Colour Eggs

Duration of Experiment: 2 hours   Difficulty Level: ▬▬ ▬▬ ▬▬

What you need:

Yellow onion skins   Pan   Eggs   Water

What to do:

Step 1. Fill $\frac{1}{4}^{th}$ of the pan with water and add the yellow onion skins.

Step 2. Boil the water, reduce the heat and let it simmer for five minutes. Take it off the heat and let it cool for 30 minutes.

Step 3. Boil the eggs in the bowl of coloured water.

Step 4. Once it comes to a boil, reduce the heat.

Step 5. Let it simmer for 20 minutes.

💡 **What just happened?** Heating the skins extracted the pigments from them. Boiling the eggs in coloured water helped transfer the dye from the water to the eggs.

61. Dancing Raisins

Duration of Experiment:  5 mins.   Difficulty Level: ▬▬ ▬▬ ▬▬

What you need:

Glass jar   Raisins   ¾ cup cooking vinegar   2 tsp. baking soda   Water

What to do:

Step 1. Fill $\frac{3}{4}^{th}$ of the jar with water.

Step 2. Add vinegar and baking soda to the jar.

Step 3. Drop 10 raisins into the jar.

Step 4. Soon, they start 'dancing' in the jar, sinking and rising.

💡 **What just happened?** The vinegar and baking soda reacted to form carbon dioxide, which stuck to surface of the raisins and carried them up. Once the gas reached the surface, it escaped into the air and the raisins sank again.

62. Fold the Egg

Duration of Experiment: ⏱ 1 week   Difficulty Level: ▬ ▬ ▬

What you need:

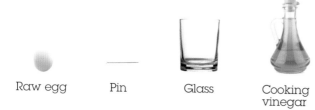

Raw egg   Pin   Glass   Cooking vinegar

What to do:

Step 1. Make two small holes on both ends of the egg. They should be about half a centimetre in diameter.

Step 2. Poke the pin through one of the holes and jiggle it around so the yolk breaks.

Step 3. Clean one end of the egg and blow into the hole so that all the liquid comes out from the other end. The egg should be completely hollow.

Step 4. Place this hollow egg in a glass full of vinegar and leave it for a week.

Step 5. After a week, squeeze the vinegar out of the egg; It should be soft and flexible now.

Step 6. Fold the egg, it becomes flat! Try tossing and bouncing it around between your hands; it regains its original round shape!

💡 **What just happened?** The acetic acid in the vinegar dissolves the calcium in the shell, which causes the shell to lose its hardness. When you fold it, the air exits the membrane through the tiny holes. Tossing it around lets air enter the membrane, allowing it to regain its shape.

63. Electric Slime

Duration of Experiment: ⏱ **20** mins. Difficulty Level: ▬▬ ▬▬ ▬

What you need:

| 3 tbsps. cornflour | 3 tbsps. vegetable oil | Balloon | Spoon | Cup |

What to do:

Step 1. Mix the vegetable oil and the cornflour in the cup. The consistency should be similar to that of thick cream.

Step 2. Blow the balloon and rub it against your hair.

Step 3. Put a bit of the mixture in the spoon and move it towards the balloon. You will notice that the mixture becomes thick and 'moves towards' the balloon.

💡 **What just happened?** Rubbing the balloon against your hair gives it a positive charge. The starch molecules in the cornflour are attracted to the balloon.

64. Dye a Cloth

Duration of Experiment: ⏱ **2** hours Difficulty Level: ▬▬ ▬▬ ▬

What you need:

| Carrot | Glass bowl | Saucepan | Strainer | Water | Cloth | Knife |

What to do:

Step 1. Put finely chopped carrot and a little water in the saucepan.

Step 2. Boil it for an hour. Add water when it dries up.

Step 3. Strain the liquid into a glass bowl, wipe the pan clean and pour the dye back.

Step 4. Place the cloth in the pot and boil it for 10 minutes.

Step 5. Remove your coloured cloth and hang it to dry!

💡 **What just happened?** The heat causes the pigments to separate from the carrot. Heating it along with the cloth causes the pigments to colour the cloth.

65. Glowing Sugar

Duration of Experiment: ⏱ 15 mins.   Difficulty Level: ▬ ▬ ▬

What you need:

Sugar lumps   Pliers

What to do:

Step 1. Take the sugar lumps to a dark room.

Step 2. Crush them with the pliers.

Step 3. You will be able to see small flashes of blue-green sparks.

💡 **What just happened?** When sugar crystals break, sometimes, one side has more positive charge that the other. When you crush the lumps, you are pulling apart the positive and the negative charges. This gives off enough energy to make it spark.

 ## 66. Invisible Fire Extinguisher

Duration of Experiment: ⏱ 10 mins.   Difficulty Level: ▬ ▬ ▬

What you need:

4 tsp. baking soda   Candle   2 tsp. cooking vinegar   Cup   Matchsticks

What to do:

Step 1. Mix the baking soda and vinegar in the cup.

Step 2. Let the mixture stop fizzing and light the candle.

Step 3. Pretend that there is a liquid in the glass and 'pour' it over the candle to magically snuff the flame out!

💡 **What just happened?** The baking soda and vinegar reacted to form carbon dioxide. Fire needs oxygen to burn. When you 'poured' the carbon dioxide onto the flame, the flame did not get any oxygen and so it died.

67. Vinegar Mix

Duration of Experiment: 5 mins.   Difficulty Level:

What you need:

3 tsp. mustard

Salt

3 tsp. cooking vinegar

3 tsp. oil

Glasses

What to do:

Step 1. Pour vinegar, oil, mustard and a pinch of salt in one glass.

Step 2. In the second, mix vinegar, mustard and a pinch of salt. Add oil while mixing.

Step 3. In the third, mix oil, vinegar and a pinch of salt.

Step 4. Try to observe the best mix.

What just happened? In the first glass, the oil forms small bubbles in the vinegar. In the second and third glasses, the oil and vinegar don't mix. Oil and vinegar don't mix unless the mustard helps bind it.

68. Fruity Fireball

Duration of Experiment: 5 mins.   Difficulty Level:

What you need:

Candle

Orange peel

Matchsticks

What to do:

Step 1. Light the candle.

Step 2. Hold the orange peel next to the candle and squeeze it.

Step 3. Your candle will burst into an impressive fireball as the droplets from the peel fly towards the flame.

> Be careful while handling fire and make sure your hands don't get too close to the flame.

What just happened? There are small compartments in an orange peel that are filled with oil. When you squeeze the peel, these compartments also get squeezed and spray the oil in the direction of the candle, which flames up.

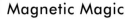

MAGNETIC MAGIC

Experiments on the principle of magnetism

I bet you must have played with magnets at some point of time. But you probably didn't know that the first magnet was discovered by a poor shepherd boy named Magnes more than three thousand years ago!

All magnets have a North Pole and a South Pole. And as they say, opposites attract. This applies to magnets as well. The North Pole of one magnet will be attracted to only the South Pole of another magnet and repelled by its North Pole.

Another interesting property of magnets is that the North Pole of a magnet, when suspended freely, always points towards the North!

69. Magnetic Pick Up

Duration of Experiment: ⏱ 5 mins.   Difficulty Level: ▬ ▬ ▬

What you need:

Paper	Paper clip	Thread	Tape	Scissors	Magnet	Table

What to do:

Step 1. Cut a three inch paper in the shape of a kite. Attach a paper clip to one corner.

Step 2. Tape a piece of thread on the opposite corner.

Step 3. Tape the other end of the thread to a table.

Step 4. Hold the magnet near the paper clip. Watch the kite 'fly'.

💡 **What just happened?** Magnets have a magnetic field, an invisible force that attracts some kinds of metal. Metal objects within the magnetic field do not have to touch a magnet to be pulled by magnetism.

70. Oily

Duration of Experiment: ⏱ 5 mins. Difficulty Level: ▬ ▬ ▬ ▬

What you need:

Magnet   Bottle   5 nails   Oil

What to do:

Step 1. Fill half the bottle with oil and drop the nails in it.

Step 2. Hold a magnet outside the bottle.

Step 3. Watch the nails jump through the oil towards the magnet.

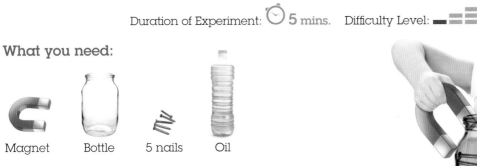

💡 **What just happened?** Magnets retain their properties even through oil.

71. Find the North

Duration of Experiment: ⏱ 15 mins. Difficulty Level: ▬ ▬ ▬ ▬

What you need:

Magnet   String   Compass

What to do:

Step 1. Tie a loop around the centre of the magnet with the string. Suspend the magnet by holding the string.

Step 2. Wait till it settles in one position.

Step 3. With the help of a compass, see which end of the magnet is pointing North. Mark it 'S'. This is the South Pole of the magnet, which will always be attracted to the North Pole of the Earth.

Step 4. Simply suspend the magnet anytime; 'S' will always point to the North.

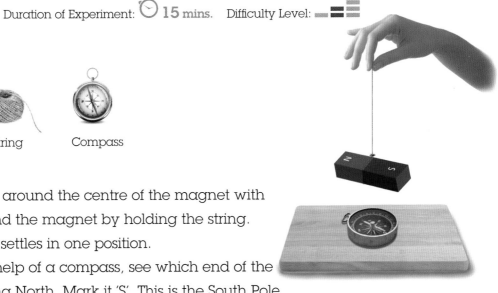

💡 **What just happened?** One end of every magnet is called the North Pole and the other, the South. The North Pole of the magnet is always attracted to the South Pole of the Earth and vice versa.

72. Make an Electromagnet

Duration of Experiment: 15 mins.   Difficulty Level: ▬ ▬ ▬

What you need:

Iron nail   Battery   Thin coated copper wire   Paper clips   Scissors

What to do:

Step 1. Leave about eight inches of wire loose at one end and wrap the rest of it around the nail. Try not to let the wire overlap.

Step 2. Cut the wire so that there are another eight inches loose at the other end too.

Step 3. Now, remove an inch of the plastic coating from both ends of the wire. Attach one wire to one end of a battery and the other wire to the other end.

Step 4. Put the point of the nail near a few paper clips; it should pick them up!

💡 **What just happened?** The electricity flowing through the wire arranges the molecules in the nail so that they are attracted to certain metals.

73. Hanging Compass

Duration of Experiment: 🕐 15 mins. Difficulty Level:

What you need:

Pencil   Thread   Large needle   Magnet

What to do:

Step 1. Stroke the needle with one end of the magnet several times.

Step 2. Tie the needle to the pencil using the thread, as shown in the image.

Step 3. Walk around and watch your needle point to the magnetic North!

💡 **What just happened?** By rubbing the needle against the magnet, the needle began to act like a magnet.

74. Make a Compass

Duration of Experiment: 🕐 15 mins. Difficulty Level:

What you need:

Horseshoe magnet   Clay   Pencil

What to do:

Step 1. Mould the clay to form a mound.

Step 2. Stick the pencil into this mound with the pointy end on top.

Step 3. Balance the magnet on the pointy end and let it settle in the north-south direction.

💡 **What just happened?** One end of every magnet is called the North Pole and the other, the South. The North Pole of the magnet is always attracted to the South Pole of the Earth.

75. Fun With Magnets

Duration of Experiment: 🕐 10 mins.   Difficulty Level: ▬▬ ▬▬ ▬▬

What you need:

Salt   Chalk powder   Plastic bottle   Magnet   Paper clips

What to do:

Step 1. Add an equal amount of coloured chalk powder and salt in a bottle.

Step 2. Add the paper clips and shake the bottle.

Step 3. Hold up a magnet to the bottle and watch the paper clips jump up towards the magnet!

💡 **What just happened?** The metallic objects were attracted to the magnet, but the salt and chalk was not. Only metals are attracted to magnets. That is why the clips 'jumped' out through the salt and chalk.

76. Make a Magnet Painting

Duration of Experiment: 🕐 15 mins.   Difficulty Level: ▬▬ ▬▬ ▬▬

What you need:

Paper plate   Magnet   Paper clips   Poster paint

What to do:

Step 1. Squirt different coloured paints onto the plate.

Step 2. Place the paper clips on the plate.

Step 3. Hold the magnet under the plate and guide the clip through the paint.

💡 **What just happened?** The paper clip is attracted to the magnet. When you move the magnet, you move the paper clip along with it, creating a metal 'paintbrush'.

77. Hot Magnets

Duration of Experiment: ⏱ **25** mins. Difficulty Level: ▬ ▬ ▬

What you need:

Needle   Compass   Magnet   Pliers

What to do:

Step 1. Use the bar magnet to magnetise the needle. This can be done by stroking the needle with the bar magnet in the same direction several times.

Step 2. Hold it near a compass. You will see the compass needle move.

Step 3. Hold the needle over a hot stove with the help of the pliers.

Step 4. Hold it there for 20 minutes.

Step 5. Now, take it off the flame and hold it near the compass. It will have no effect.

Why does a magnet lose its magnetism?

You can imagine a magnet as a bunch of tiny particles pointing in the same direction. When you heat a magnet, the little magnetic parts can get jostled and unaligned, destroying magnetism.

⚠ Be careful while heating the magnet. Always make sure that there is an adult around to supervise when you use fire.

💡 **What just happened?** The first time you held the needle near the compass, the needle was magnetised and made the compass needle move. After heating, it lost its magnetic properties and had no effect on the compass.

78. Extract Iron from Your Cereal

Duration of Experiment: 15 mins.   Difficulty Level:

What you need:

Cornflakes

Bowl and spoon

Magnet

White paper

What to do:

Step 1. Crush your cereal in your bowl with the help of your spoon until it becomes a powder.

Step 2. Pour this powder onto the white paper.

Step 3. Run your magnet over it.

Step 4. You should be able to pick up tiny black particles.

Step 5. These are actually little bits of iron in your cereal!

💡 **What just happened?** Iron is a mineral that is necessary for our survival in small proportions. It is also magnetic and so gets picked up with the magnet.

79. Magnetic Poles

Duration of Experiment: 🕐 5 mins.   Difficulty Level: ▬ ▬ ▬

What you need:

Iron fillings

Magnet

White paper

What to do:

Step 1. Place the bar magnet on the piece of paper.

Step 2. Sprinkle the iron fillings around the magnet.

Step 3. Try to see where there are maximum iron fillings.

Step 4. Most of the fillings are attracted to the two ends or poles.

💡 **What just happened?** Each magnet has a magnetic field or an area where its force is felt. This field or area of influence is strongest at the two poles.

80. Read a Credit Card

Duration of Experiment: ⏱ 10 mins.   Difficulty Level: ▬ ▬ ▬

What you need:

Old credit card

Rusted nail

Sandpaper

What to do:

Step 1. Scrape some rusty powder off the nail with the sandpaper.

Step 2. Pour this rust over the magnetic strip of the card.

Step 3. Tap off the excess rust. Look at the strip under uniform white light.

Step 4. Some black particles from the rust will be stuck to the magnetic strip.

💡 **What just happened?** The magnetic strip on a credit card stores its information magnetically, so areas of the strip will be magnetised. The black particles from rust contain iron, which is attracted to the magnetic strip.

81. All Uphill

Duration of Experiment: ⏱ 5 mins.   Difficulty Level: ▬ ▬ ▬

What you need:

Magnet

Paper clip

Cardboard

What to do:

Step 1. Fold the bottom of the cardboard and make it stand at a slight inclination.

Step 2. Place the paper clip at the bottom.

Step 3. Place your magnet behind the cardboard and guide the paper clip uphill.

💡 **What just happened?** Magnetic force works even through non-magnetic materials like cardboard.

82. From Outer Space

Duration of Experiment: 30 mins.   Difficulty Level:

What you need:

Magnet   Paper   Jar

What to do:

Step 1. Collect dust from different locations of your house in a jar.

Step 2. Pour this dust onto the white paper.

Step 3. Hold the magnet beneath the paper and tap the paper so that all the dust is on top on the magnet.

Step 4. Tilt the paper while keeping the magnet stationary. Some dust particles will be attracted to the magnet.

What just happened? Tons of space dust and debris blast the Earth everyday. Most perish in the atmosphere, but the few that survive are magnetic in nature.

83. Car Racing

Duration of Experiment: 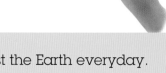 15 mins.   Difficulty Level:

What you need:

Toy cars   Rubber bands   Magnet

What to do:

Step 1. Use the rubber bands to attach one bar magnet under each of the cars.

Step 2. The North Pole should be facing the back of one car and the front of the other.

Step 3. Put the two cars one behind the other and see if you can 'push' the car in front without touching it.

What just happened? Similar poles of magnets repel each other.

84. Chain Reaction

Duration of Experiment: 5 mins.   Difficulty Level: ▬ ▬ ▬

What you need:

Magnet   Nails

What to do:

Step 1. Hang a nail on the magnet.

Step 2. Use this nail to pick up other nails.

Step 3. See how many nails you can get to join your chain!

What just happened? Magnets can 'magnetise' or give magnetic properties to metals that are touching them. As long the nail is touching the magnet, it acts as a weaker magnet, attracting the next nail.

85. Wrapped Magnets

Duration of Experiment: 5 mins.   Difficulty Level: ▬ ▬ ▬

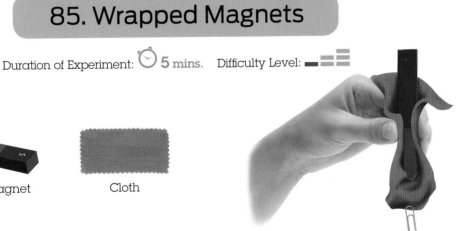

What you need:

Paper clips   Magnet   Cloth

What to do:

Step 1. Wrap the magnet in cloth.

Step 2. Try to attract the paper clips. They will be easily attracted.

Step 3. Wrap the magnet in another layer of cloth and see if the clips are still attracted. How many cloths does it take for the magnet to stop being effective?

What just happened? Magnets retain their magnetism even through material like cloth, as long as it is not too thick. Thicker materials prevent the magnet from exerting its force.

86. Snake Charmer

Duration of Experiment: ⏱ 5 mins.   Difficulty Level: ▬ ▬ ▬

What you need:

Bunch of keys   Thin rope   Magnet   Tape   Table

What to do:

Step 1. Tie one end of the thin rope to the keys.

Step 2. Tape the other end to the table.

Step 3. Use the magnet to guide the keys without touching them.

💡 **What just happened?** There is an area around the magnet called the magnetic field, where the magnet's force can be felt. The keys need not be in contact with the magnet to be attracted to it.

87. Levitation

Duration of Experiment: ⏱ 15 mins.   Difficulty Level: ▬ ▬ ▬

What you need:

Scissors   Card paper   Tape   Round magnets

What to do:

Step 1. Make a tube shape out of the card paper and tape it. The diameter should be slightly larger than the round magnets.

Step 2. Slit the side of the tube so that you can look inside clearly.

Step 3. Put both magnets in the tube with both north poles facing each other.

Step 4. Look at the levitating magnet through the slit!

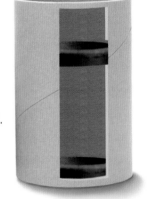

💡 **What just happened?** Similar poles of magnets repel each other. The repulsion caused one magnet to levitate.

88. Make a Compass

Duration of Experiment: ⏱ 15 mins.   Difficulty Level: ▬ ▬ ▬

What you need:

Needle   Cork   Pen   Magnet   Bowl   Compass   Knife   Water

What to do:

Step 1. Stroke the needle with the magnet in the same direction multiple times. This will magnetise the needle.

Step 2. Cut a 1.5 cm slice from the cork.

Step 3. Push the needle in through the diameter.

Step 4. Fill the bowl half with water.

Step 5. Place the cork in the water. It will spin till one end of the needle points to the North.

Step 6. Use the compass to figure out which end is pointing to the North.

Step 7. Mark the North, South, East and West respectively.

SCIENCE AROUND US

Discovery of Magnets

Legend says that a shepherd named Magnes discovered natural magnets 3,000 years ago. He was herding his sheep when the nails on his shoes and the metal tip of his staff suddenly got stuck to the rock he was standing on.

💡 **What just happened?** Rubbing the needle with the magnet 'magnetised' it or gave it the properties of a magnet. We know that we can use magnets to find out which direction the North lies in.

89. Floating Magnets

Duration of Experiment: ⏱ 15 mins.   Difficulty Level: ▬ ▬ ▬

What you need:

7 corks   7 needles   Magnet   Container   Water

What to do:

Step 1. Fill the container with water.

Step 2. Place all the needles together in a row. Make sure they are all facing the same direction.

Step 3. Magnetise them by stroking them with one pole of a magnet.

Step 4. Push the needles through the top of the corks. Let only a little bit of the eye stick out.

Step 5. Place these in the container.

Step 6. Hold a magnet over it and watch the needles form patterns.

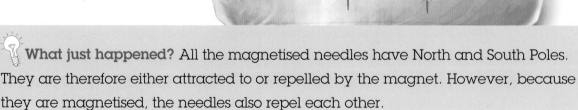

💡 **What just happened?** All the magnetised needles have North and South Poles. They are therefore either attracted to or repelled by the magnet. However, because they are magnetised, the needles also repel each other.

90. Magnetic Race Track

Duration of Experiment: ⏱ 15 mins.   Difficulty Level: ▬ ▬ ▬

What you need:

Cardboard

Toy car

Pencil

Magnets

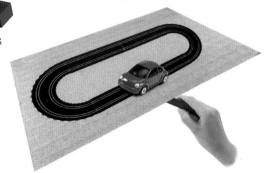

What to do:

Step 1. Draw a racetrack on the cardboard.

Step 2. Place the magnet under the car.

Step 3. Hold another magnet under the cardboard and use it to guide the car through the racetrack.

💡 **What just happened?** Magnetic attraction works even through the cardboard. That is why you were able to guide the car with the magnet.

91. Lines of Force

Duration of Experiment: ⏱ 5 mins.   Difficulty Level: ▬ ▬ ▬

What you need:

Horseshoe magnet

Iron fillings

Papers

Clay slab

What to do:

Step 1. Mould the clay around the magnet such that the magnet can stand with its poles facing upward without support.

Step 2. Place the paper horizontally across the poles.

Step 3. Sprinkle iron fillings on the paper.

Step 4. Watch the fillings arrange themselves into a fascinating pattern.

💡 **What just happened?** The iron fillings arrange themselves along the 'lines of force'. These are imaginary lines that show the direction of the magnet's attraction.

GETTING HOT IN HERE

Experiments on the principle of heat

Just like you get irritable and cranky when the weather is too hot, heat can have an interesting effect on other substances too.

When air is heated, it expands and rises. Though this seems rather unimpressive, this property of air can be used in many fascinating ways, as you will learn in this section.

Also learn how to elude the wrath of fire by making fireproof balloons, handkerchiefs and paper vessels!

Once again, remember that fire can be very dangerous and adult supervision is strongly recommended for all experiments that involve the use of fire.

92. Fireproof Balloons

Duration of Experiment: 🕐 15 mins.   Difficulty Level:

What you need:

Balloons

Matchsticks

¼ cup water

What to do:

Step 1. Put water in a balloon. Inflate and tie it.

Step 2. Inflate the other balloon without the water.

Step 3. Hold a lit matchstick under the balloon that does not have water. It will burst.

Step 4. Now, hold a lit matchstick under the balloon with water. It won't burst.

💡 **What just happened?** The water absorbs most of the heat in the case of the second balloon. This is why the water inside the balloon becomes hot, but the balloon does not burst.

93. Black or White?

Duration of Experiment: **45** mins.   Difficulty Level: ▬▬ ▬ ▬

What you need:

Glasses   Water   Thermometer   Rubber bands   White and
Black paper

What to do:

Step 1. Wrap one glass with white paper and the other with black paper. Secure both of them with the rubber bands.

Step 2. Fill both glasses halfway with water.

Step 3. Leave them in the sunlight for half an hour.

Step 4. Measure the temperature of both. The black glass will be warmer.

💡 **What just happened?** Dark surfaces such as the black paper absorb more light and heat than the lighter ones such as the white paper.

94. Levitating Spiral

Duration of Experiment: **10** mins.   Difficulty Level: ▬▬ ▬ ▬

What you need:

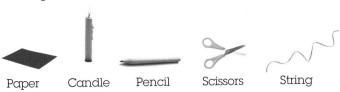

Paper   Candle   Pencil   Scissors   String

What to do:

Step 1. Draw a thin spiral on a piece of paper and cut it out.

Step 2. Light the candle.

Step 3. Tie the spiral to the pencil using the string. Hold this over the candle.

Step 4. Watch as the paper rises by itself.

❗ Don't hold the spiral too close to the flame. It could catch fire.

💡 **What just happened?** The air around the candle gets heated. As the air gets warmer, it expands and becomes lighter. It rises. Since the spiral is light, it rises along with the air.

95. Sticky Glasses

Duration of Experiment: 5 mins.   Difficulty Level:

What you need:

2 plastic glasses   Paper towel   Hot water

What to do:

Step 1. Wet the paper towel with the hot water, but don't crumple it.

Step 2. Fill one of the plastic glasses with hot water and pour it out.

Step 3. Lay the paper on top of this glass.

Step 4. Pour some water into the other glass and pour it out.

Step 5. Turn this glass over and put it on top of the paper towel.

Step 6. Hold it there for 30 seconds and pick it up. You will find that both glasses are stuck to each other.

What is heat energy?

Heat energy is the term used to describe the level of activity in the molecules of an object. The Sun is the primary source of heat energy in our solar system.

What just happened? When you pour the hot water into the glasses, it heats the air inside, which expands. Once the air starts cooling, the pressure reduces, but new air cannot enter the glasses because they are stuck together. The pressure from the air outside keeps the glasses firmly stuck to each other.

96. The Talking Coin

Duration of Experiment: 20 mins.   Difficulty Level:

What you need:

Coin   Plastic bottle   Water

What to do:

Step 1. Put the empty bottle in the freezer for 15 minutes.

Step 2. Wet the coin.

Step 3. Take the bottle out and put it on a table.

Step 4. Quickly put the wet coin over the mouth of the bottle.

Step 5. Watch the coin bob up and down, as if it's talking.

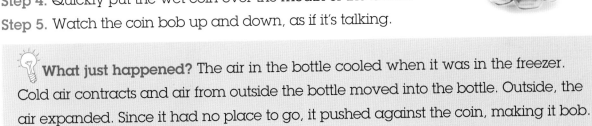

What just happened? The air in the bottle cooled when it was in the freezer. Cold air contracts and air from outside the bottle moved into the bottle. Outside, the air expanded. Since it had no place to go, it pushed against the coin, making it bob.

97. Fireproof Handkerchief

Duration of Experiment: 5 mins.   Difficulty Level:

What you need:

Coin   Handkerchief   Matchsticks

What to do:

Step 1. Stretch a handkerchief over a coin and tie it.

Step 2. Light a match and hold it against the handkerchief pulled over the coin.

Step 3. You will be surprised to see that the cloth does not burn!

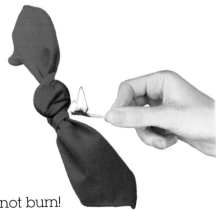

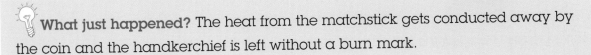

What just happened? The heat from the matchstick gets conducted away by the coin and the handkerchief is left without a burn mark.

98. Ahoy There!

Duration of Experiment: ⏱ 1 hour   Difficulty Level: ▬▬ ▬▬ ▬▬

What you need:

Metal tube   Clothes hanger   Candles   Plywood   Masking tape   Tub   Water

Saw   Cork   Nails

What to do:

Step 1. Shut both ends of the tube with the cork.

Step 2. Poke a hole in one of the corks with a nail.

Step 3. Cut the plywood in the shape of a boat for the base.

Step 4. Use the hangers to attach the tube to the boat. Place the hangers vertically such that the tube is held in the hooks of the hanger and there is sufficient place for the candles to be placed below it.

Step 5. Stick the two candles near the edges of the board. Use loops of masking tape to stick the candles to the wood.

Step 6. Hammer two nails vertically opposite each other at the ends of the 'boat'. The nails will help stabilise the structure.

Step 7. Replace the cork.

Step 8. Light the candles and set it in a tub of water.

Step 9. Watch your steamboat go!

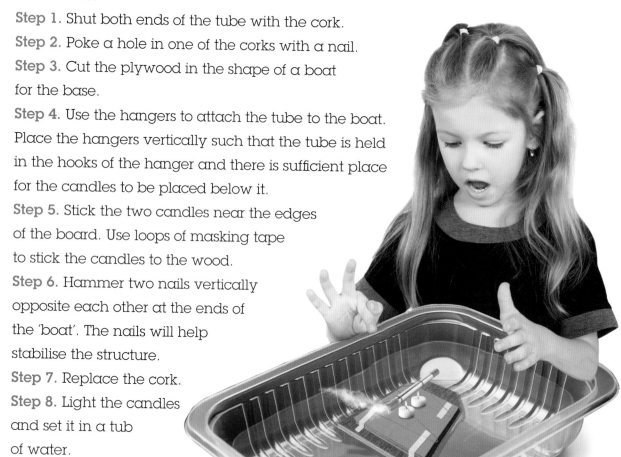

💡 **What just happened?** The candle causes the water to boil. This creates steam that escapes through the hole in the cork, pushing the boat forward.

99. Hot or Cold?

Duration of Experiment: ⏱ **40** mins.   Difficulty Level: ▬ ▬ ▬

What you need:

Thermometer

Thermocol sheet

Metal sheet

What to do:

Step 1. Place the metal sheet and the thermocol in a room for at least 30 minutes.

Step 2. Touch both the sheets with two different hands. Which one feels cooler?

Step 3. Now, use the thermometer to measure their temperatures. They will both be the same.

💡 **What just happened?** Though both the materials are at the same temperature, the rate at which they take heat away from your body differs. Therefore, the metal seems colder than the thermocol.

100. Chocolate Leaves

Duration of Experiment: ⏱ **25** mins.   Difficulty Level: ▬ ▬ ▬

What you need:

Leaves

Clean paintbrush

Chocolate

Microwave-
safe bowl

Water

What to do:

Step 1. Wash and dry the leaves carefully.

Step 2. Place the chocolate in a microwave-safe bowl. Heat it till the chocolate melts on half power.

Step 3. Once it is a thick liquid, use the brush to paint the leaves on only one side.

Step 4. Put it in the fridge. Once it is solid, peel the leaf off. The chocolate retains the shape of the leaf!

💡 **What just happened?** On raising the temperature, the solid chocolate becomes liquid. When you put it in the fridge, it solidifies again, retaining the new shape.

101. Paper Vessel

Duration of Experiment: 30 mins.   Difficulty Level: ▬ ▬ ▬

What you need:

Sheet of stiff paper   Cardboard   Paper clips   Water
                              box

What to do:

Step 1. Cover the cardboard box with the stiff paper using the paper clips to support it.

Step 2. Fill the vessel with water and hold it over the stove.

Step 3. In a while, you will see that the water starts boiling without the paper catching fire!

> ⓘ Fire can be dangerous. Make sure there is an adult around while performing this experiment.

💡 **What just happened?** While heating, the water draws the heat away from the paper. Thus, all the heat is absorbed by the water and the paper does not catch fire.

102. Hot Rubber

Duration of Experiment: ⏲ 5 mins.   Difficulty Level: ▬ ▬ ▬

What you need:

Rubber band   Hair dryer   Small plastic toy   Doorknob   Pencil

What to do:

Step 1. Attach the toy to one end of the rubber band and hang it on a doorknob.

Step 2. With the pencil, mark where it reaches on the door.

Step 3. Using the hair dryer, heat the rubber band.

Step 4. After three minutes, you will notice that the toy has risen from its earlier position.

💡 **What just happened?** Unlike most materials, rubber contracts when heated. This causes the toy to rise up as well.

ALL FALL DOWN

Experiments on the principle of gravity

You've probably heard of Newton and how he discovered gravity when an apple fell on his head. In this section, you can do your own little experiments to prove his theory.

You can also study certain processes that 'defy' gravity, like capillary action and the centrifugal force.

You will also learn how to balance a rather large number of irregularly shaped objects using the principle of 'centre of gravity'.

103. Anti-gravity Water

Duration of Experiment: 5 mins.   Difficulty Level:

What you need:

Glass   Cardboard   Water

What to do:

Step 1. Fill the glass to the brim with water.

Step 2. Cover it with the cardboard. Make sure that no air bubbles enter the glass.

Step 3. Hold the cardboard and turn the glass upside down, preferably over a sink.

Step 4. Now move your hand away from the cardboard. The cardboard remains in place, defying gravity.

💡 **What just happened?** By not allowing any air to enter the glass, you made sure that the air pressure outside the glass was greater than the air pressure inside. This helped keep the cardboard in place.

104. Magical Water

Duration of Experiment: 🕐 2 hours   Difficulty Level: ▬ ▬ ▬

What you need:

Glasses   Yellow and blue paint   Paper towels   Water

What to do:

Step 1. Fill two glasses with water.

Step 2. Put blue paint in one and yellow in the other.

Step 3. Place the empty glass between the two.

Step 4. Twist the paper towels together and set them up as shown.

Step 5. You will soon see the empty glass filling up with green water!

💡 **What just happened?** By a process called capillary action, the water uses the tiny gaps between the fibres of the paper towels to move along. When the yellow and blue paint mix in the empty glass, it forms green water.

105. Dual Coloured Flowers

Duration of Experiment: 🕐 48 hours   Difficulty Level: ▬ ▬ ▬

What you need:

Coloured ink   White flower   Glasses   Knife   Water

What to do:

Step 1. Slit the stem of the flower vertically with the knife.

Step 2. Mix different coloured inks and water in each glass.

Step 3. Put one half of the stem in one glass and the other half in the other glass.

Step 4. In a few hours, the petals of your flower will appear dual coloured!

💡 **What just happened?** The water travels up the stem of the plant into the leaves and flowers, where it makes food. This process is called 'capillary action'.

106. Rolly Polly Doll

Duration of Experiment: ⏱ 30 mins.   Difficulty Level: ▬ ▬ ▬

What you need:

Bouncy ball   Knife   Pencil   Paper   Scotch tape   Scissors

What to do:

Step 1. Cut the bouncy ball in half.

Step 2. Place it on a table with the flat side facing up.

Step 3. Draw a 10 cm × 10 cm square on the paper. Cut it out.

Step 4. Roll the square paper to form a tube. Tape it to the cut ball.
The round part of the ball should stick out from the bottom.

Step 5. Keep cutting small sections off the top of the paper tube till the
tube returns to an upright position when it's knocked over.

Step 6. Draw a clown on the paper tube
and play with your toy.

💡 **What just happened?** The centre of gravity for an object is the point at which
the object's average weight is located. If you support the centre of gravity, you
support the entire object. When you cut this ball in half there is a shift in the centre
of gravity and the object loses its support, which causes the toy to return to an
upright position after being knocked over.

107. Colourful Blacks

Duration of Experiment: 2 hours   Difficulty Level:

What you need:

Blotting paper   Glass   Scotch tape   Ice cream stick   Black felt pens   Water

What to do:

Step 1. Draw two black lines on the bottom of two thin strips of blotting paper.

Step 2. Tape the strips to the ice cream stick with the black line at the bottom.

Step 3. Place the stick across the glass.

Step 4. Pour enough water into the glass to touch the bottom of the blotting paper, but not the black line.

Step 5. Take the blotting paper out once the water reaches the top of the blotting paper and dry it.

Step 6. You can see all the colours that black is made of.

SCIENCE AROUND US

Chromatography

In chemistry, chromatography is a process used by scientists to separate the various components of a mixture. Though scientists use more complicated apparatus and put the mixture through many steps, the experiment you just performed is an elementary form of chromatology!

What just happened? The water moved up the filter paper (against the force of gravity) through capillary action due to the tiny pores or tubes on the paper. As the water moved over the black pen lines, some chemicals dissolved better in water and spread up the blotting paper, creating a unique pattern.

108. Parachute

Duration of Experiment: ⏱ 30 mins.   Difficulty Level: ▬ ▬ ▬

What you need:

Scissors

String

Small toy

Plastic bag

What to do:

Step 1. Cut out an octagon from the plastic bag.

Step 2. Cut a small hole near the edge of each side.

Step 3. Attach eight pieces of equal-sized string to each of the holes.

Step 4. Tie the pieces of string to the toy and drop your parachute slowly.

💡 **What just happened?** When you release the parachute, the weight pulls down on the strings and opens up a large surface area of material that uses air resistance to slow it down.

109. The High Dive

Duration of Experiment: ⏱ 15 mins.   Difficulty Level: ▬ ▬ ▬

What you need:

Coin

Card paper

Film canister

Pencil

Scissors

Water

What to do:

Step 1. Cut the card paper into a long strip to form a hoop.

Step 2. Put a little water in the canister. Place the hoop on the film canister and balance the coin on it.

Step 3. In one swift motion, use the pencil to fling the hoop off to the side.

Step 4. The penny will fall straight into the canister with a splash.

💡 **What just happened?** When you swiftly got the hoop out of the way, the penny was left suspended over the film canister with nothing to hold it up. Gravity caused it to fall straight into the canister.

110. Colour Changing Carnations

Duration of Experiment: **48** hours   Difficulty Level:

What you need:

Knife   3 white carnations   Food colouring   Water   3 glasses of water

What to do:

Step 1. Fill half of each glass with water. Add 30 drops of food colouring into three different glasses.

Step 2. Make a fresh diagonal cut at the end of each stem and place each one on a different glass.

Step 3. Within two days, the colour of the carnation petals will change.

What just happened? The water travels up the stem of the plant into the leaves and flowers, where it makes food. This process is called capillary action.

111. Spinning Bucket

Duration of Experiment: **5** mins.   Difficulty Level:

What you need:

Water   Bucket

What to do:

Step 1. Fill half the bucket with water. Place its handle in the crook of your arm and spin it in a circular motion.

Step 2. If you spin it fast enough, the water will remain in the bucket even when it is upside down.

What just happened? This experiment uses 'centripetal force'. This force ensures that an object continues travelling in a circular path with a fixed centre.

112. Swing King

Duration of Experiment: ⏱ 5 mins.   Difficulty Level: ▬▬ ▬▬ ▬▬

What you need:

Watch

Swing

What to do:

Step 1. Hold the seat of the swing and move behind by 2–3 steps. Form a mark in the ground in front of your feet.

Step 2. Leave the swing without pushing it. Count the number of times the swing goes back and forth in 10 seconds. Your friend can help you keep time.

Step 3. Now, ask your friend to sit on the swing.

Step 4. Pull the swing back to the exact position it was in earlier. (You can do this with the help of the mark you made on the ground earlier.)

Step 5. Leave the swing like before and count how many times it goes back and forth. It will be the same with and without your friend.

SCIENCE AROUND US

Pendulums

Pendulums are designed such that once they start moving, they keep moving. The basic force that makes a pendulum move is gravity. However, the pendulums in clocks use a complex system of gears to keep it ticking.

💡 **What just happened?** The swing moves because of gravity's force. This gravitational force does not change if the weight differs.

113. Candle Seesaw

Duration of Experiment: ⏱ **5** mins.   Difficulty Level: ▬ ▬ ▬

What you need:

Needle   Glasses   Candle   Knife

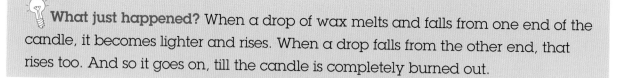

What to do:

Step 1. Scrape the wax off one end of the candle. Make sure that the wick is exposed.

Step 2. Push a long needle into the middle of the candle.

Step 3. Balance this on the two glasses.

Step 4. Light both ends of candle.

💡 **What just happened?** When a drop of wax melts and falls from one end of the candle, it becomes lighter and rises. When a drop falls from the other end, that rises too. And so it goes on, till the candle is completely burned out.

114. Upright Broom

Duration of Experiment: ⏱ **30** mins.   Difficulty Level: ▬ ▬ ▬

What you need:

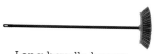

Long handle broom

What to do:

Step 1. Find a smooth, hard floor. Place the broom on the floor with the bristles facing down.

Step 2. Keep adjusting the handle by pushing it slightly forward or backward till you can get it to stand on its own.

💡 **What just happened?** By making slight adjustments to the handle, you shifted the centre of gravity till it was ideal for the broom to balance without support.

115. Spinning

Duration of Experiment: ⏱ 15 mins.   Difficulty Level: ▬ ▬ ▬

What you need:

Small rubber ball

Jar

Table

What to do:

Step 1. Put the ball on the table and put the jar over it.

Step 2. Slowly begin spinning the ball in the jar.

Step 3. Increase your speed slowly and lift the jar off the table.

Step 4. The ball will also get picked up.

💡 **What just happened?** The ball is forced to keep spinning in the jar due to a force known as 'centripetal force'. This ensures that the ball keeps spinning, even when gravity is acting against it.

116. Anti-gravity Machine

Duration of Experiment: ⏱ 30 mins.   Difficulty Level: ▬ ▬ ▬

What you need:

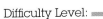

Tape

Long rulers

2 plastic funnels of the same size

Thick books

What to do:

Step 1. Tape the two funnels together and set up the rest of the apparatus as shown in the picture.

Step 2. Place the funnels at the 'bottom' (narrower end) of the slope. Watch as it rolls up towards the higher pile!

💡 **What just happened?** Though it seems as if the funnel is climbing the slope, it is actually moving down towards the table, thanks to its centre of gravity.

117. Balancing it

Duration of Experiment: ⏱ 30 mins.   Difficulty Level: ▬ ▬ ▬

What you need:

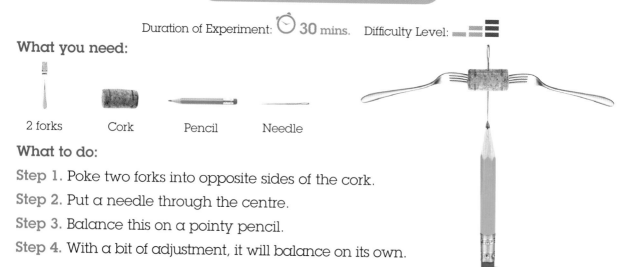

2 forks   Cork   Pencil   Needle

What to do:

Step 1. Poke two forks into opposite sides of the cork.

Step 2. Put a needle through the centre.

Step 3. Balance this on a pointy pencil.

Step 4. With a bit of adjustment, it will balance on its own.

💡 **What just happened?** By adjusting it, you shifted the centre of gravity to make it perfect for the balancing act.

118. Anti-gravity Water

Duration of Experiment: ⏱ 5 mins.   Difficulty Level: ▬ ▬ ▬

What you need:

Glass   Handkerchief   Water

What to do:

Step 1. Place the handkerchief over the glass.

Step 2. Fill $\frac{3^{th}}{4}$ of the glass by pouring water into the middle of the handkerchief.

Step 3. Stretch the handkerchief over the glass.

Step 4. Place one hand on top of the glass and turn it.

Step 5. Remove your hand. The water should stay.

💡 **What just happened?** When you stretch out the handkerchief, the tiny holes literally disappear, allowing the molecules to bond with other water molecules, creating 'surface tension'.

119. The Merry-go-round

Duration of Experiment: **30** mins.   Difficulty Level: ▬ ▬ ≡

What you need:

Needle   3 corks   Bottle   Aluminium plate   Forks   Knife

What to do:

Step 1. Slice the corks down the middle and stick a fork, at slightly less that 90° into each slice.

Step 2. Balance these on the edge of the plate.

Step 3. Push a cork into the bottle and a needle into the cork.

Step 4. Carefully balance the plate on the needle. With a little trial and error, you can make it stay.

💡 **What just happened?** When you balance the objects on an irregularly shaped object perfectly, you have found the centre of gravity for those objects.

120. Clean Water

Duration of Experiment: **2** hours   Difficulty Level: ▬ ≡ ≡

What you need:

Woollen string   2 bowls   Dirty water   Thick books

What to do:

Step 1. Stack 3-4 books on a table and place a bowl of dirty water on it.

Step 2. Place an empty bowl next to the books.

Step 3. Put one end of the wool in the dirty water and the other in the empty bowl.

Step 4. After a while, you will see clean drops of water dripping into the empty bowl.

💡 **What just happened?** The rope absorbs water from the bowl, but leaves the dirt behind.

75

121. Obedient Egg

Duration of Experiment: 30 mins.   Difficulty Level: ▬ ▬ ▬

What you need:

Pin   Salt   Raw egg   Glue

What to do:

Step 1. Poke a hole in one end of the egg using the pin.

Step 2. Carefully make a slightly bigger hole in the other end by cracking it slightly.

Step 3. Blow through the pinhole so that the yolk is hollow.

Step 4. Let it dry for a while and glue the pinhole.

Step 5. Through the other end, add a pinch of salt and glue it shut too.

Step 6. Once it has dried, the egg will remain in whatever position you place it.

💡 **What just happened?** When you place the egg in a particular position, the salt settles at the bottom. The egg is heavier at the bottom and lighter on top. So it stays in the same position.

122. Tight-rope Dancing Bottle

Duration of Experiment: 15 mins.   Difficulty Level: ▬ ▬ ▬

What you need:

String   Glass bottle   Umbrella   Chalk

What to do:

Step 1. Tie the string loosely between any two posts and spread the chalk on it by rubbing against it.

Step 2. Push the handle of the umbrella into the neck of the bottle.

Step 3. Lay the bottle on the string and watch it balance.

💡 **What just happened?** The weight of the umbrella and the bottle balance each other out.

123. Balancing Act

Duration of Experiment: 5 mins.   Difficulty Level:

What you need:

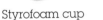

Long ruler

What to do:

Step 1. Put your hands out in front of you and balance the ruler on them.

Step 2. Now slowly move your hands closer to each other.

Step 3. The point at which both your hands meet is the centre of gravity. The ruler will balance at this point.

What just happened? Because of friction between the hand and the ruler, it is possible to determine the exact centre.

124. Falling Water

Duration of Experiment: 15 mins.   Difficulty Level:

What you need:

Styrofoam cup   Sharp pencil   Water

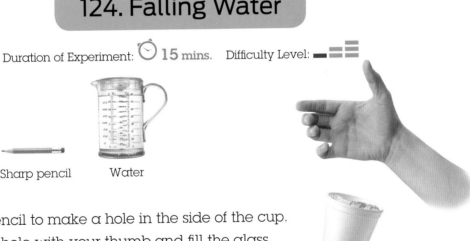

What to do:

Step 1. Use the pencil to make a hole in the side of the cup.

Step 2. Cover the hole with your thumb and fill the glass with water.

Step 3. Take your thumb off the hole. The water leaks out of the hole.

Step 4. Drop the glass. While the glass is falling, the water stops leaking from the hole.

What just happened? When you're holding the cup in your hand, gravity is pulling on the glass and the water, but only the water moves. This is because you are holding the cup in place. When you drop the glass, gravity is pulling the glass as well as the water at the same rate.

125. Disobedient Egg

Duration of Experiment: ⏱ 15 mins.   Difficulty Level: ▬ ▬ ▬

What you need:

Raw egg   Iron fillings   Pin   Glue

What to do:

Step 1. Poke a hole in one end of the egg using the pin.

Step 2. Carefully make a slightly bigger hole in the other end of the egg by cracking it slightly.

Step 3. Blow through the pinhole so that the eggshell is hollow.

Step 4. Let it dry for a while.

Step 5. Glue the pinhole shut.

Step 6. Through the other end, pour the iron fillings in.

Step 7. Pour glue over the fillings to hold them in place. Let it dry.

Step 8. Now glue the other hole shut too.

Step 9. Once it's dry, no matter what position you put it in, it will always return to its original upright position!

💡 **What just happened?** The iron fillings make the egg heavier to where it is glued. This makes the egg return to that position.

126. Balancing

Duration of Experiment: ⏱ **30** mins.   Difficulty Level: ▬▬ ▬▬ ▬

What you need:

Paper   Cup   Knives

What to do:

Step 1. Roll the paper tightly.

Step 2. Use the paper to fix two knives in the handle of the cup as shown.

Step 3. Balance the cup on your fingertip.

💡 **What just happened?** The knives help distribute the weight of the cup evenly, which makes it possible to balance.

127. Cutting Pear

Duration of Experiment: ⏱ **15** mins.   Difficulty Level: ▬▬ ▬▬ ▬

What you need:

Pear   Knife   Plate   Cup   Cotton thread   Water   Scissors

What to do:

Step 1. Tie the pear using the cotton thread. Hang it above a table.

Step 2. Fill water in the cup. Hold it under the pear so that the pear is touching the water.

Step 3. Remove the cup from under the pear. Watch where the water droplet is falling.

Step 4. Place a knife with its blade facing the spot where water droplet fell.

Step 5. Now, cut the string so that the pear falls straight on the knife and gets sliced.

💡 **What just happened?** Gravity ensured that the pear fell down in a straight line. The force with which it fell ensured that the knife sliced right through it.

128. Water Slide

Duration of Experiment: ⏱ **20** mins.   Difficulty Level:

What you need:

Plastic sheet   Different sized   Water   Saucer
                  books

What to do:

Step 1. Place several books vertically.

Step 2. Place the sheet of plastic over them, making sure there are no creases or wrinkles. Place the saucer at the end of the plastic sheet.

Step 3. Let a drop of water fall on the highest part of the slide.

Step 4. It will go down the first slope, up the second and so on till it reaches the saucer.

💡 **What just happened?** The speed that the water droplet gained on its way down the slope sustained it as it went up the next slope.

129. Race to Bottom

Duration of Experiment: ⏱ **5** mins.   Difficulty Level: ▬ ═ ═

What you need:

2 objects of different weights   Chair
(like a bottle cap and a coin)

What to do:

Step 1. Stand on a chair.

Step 2. Drop both objects at the same time.

Step 3. Try to see which one reaches the ground first.

💡 **What just happened?** Both reached at the same time! Though you may think that the heavier one would reach first, gravity exerts the same force on all objects.

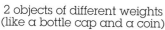

RELAX - DON'T BE DENSE!

Experiments on the principle of density

Have you ever wondered why smaller objects are sometimes heavier than larger objects? The answer lies in their 'density'. Density is the amount of matter that is packed into an object. If a bar of gold is heavier than a piece of wood of the same size, it means that gold is denser than wood.

The next time someone calls you dense, all you need to say for the perfect retort is, "Yes, I'm dense because I have extra brain cells packed in my skull".

130. Peeling the Orange

Duration of Experiment: 5 mins.   Difficulty Level:

What you need:

2 oranges   Bowl   Water

What to do:

Step 1. Fill the bowl with water.

Step 2. Peel one of the oranges.

Step 3. Place both the oranges in the bowl.

Step 4. Contrary to what you think, the orange with the peel floats while the peeled orange sinks.

What just happened? The peel of the orange is full of tiny air pockets that help give it a lower density than water, making it float to the surface. Removing the peel (and all the air pockets) from the orange increases its density, making it sink. So, even though the peeled orange is lighter than the orange with the peel, it sinks.

131. Snow Crystal

Duration of Experiment: **48** hours   Difficulty Level:

What you need:

String   Jar   Boiling water   Pipe cleaner   Sugar   Pencil   Knife

What to do:

Step 1. Cut the pipe cleaner into three equal sections.

Step 2. Shape it into a crystal.

Step 3. Tie a string to the middle of the crystal.

Step 4. Tie the opposite end to the pencil.

Step 5. Fill half the jar with boiling water.

Step 6. Keep adding sugar to the water till no more can be dissolved.

Step 7. Hang the snowflake into the jar with the pencil resting on top of it.

Step 8. Leave the snowflake overnight.

The next morning, it will be covered in crystals.

SCIENCE AROUND US

Snowflakes

Snowflakes form when water vapour in clouds condense into ice crystals. Snowflakes have a hexagonal structure, much like the sugar flake you just created! Did you know that no two snowflakes are exactly the same?

What just happened? Hot water holds more dissolved sugar than cold water. When the solution cools, the water molecules move closer together and it can't hold as much sugar as the hot water could, making the solution very dense. Crystals begin to form on top of each other and you have a crystal snowflake.

132. Floating Ketchup

Duration of Experiment: ⏱ 5 mins.   Difficulty Level: ▬ ▬ ▬

What you need:

Salt

Ketchup sachet

Plastic bottle

Water

What to do:

Step 1. Fill the plastic bottle with water and drop the ketchup sachet in it.

Step 2. Add salt to the bottle till the ketchup sachet is just about floating.

Step 3. Put the cap on and squeeze the bottle.

Step 4. The packet should sink when you squeeze it and float when you release it.

💡 **What just happened?** There is an air bubble trapped in the ketchup sachet, which makes it float. Squeezing the bottle reduces the size of the air bubble, making it sink. Once the bottle is released, the air bubble expands, making it float again.

133. The Lava Cup

Duration of Experiment: ⏱ 15 mins.   Difficulty Level: ▬ ▬ ▬

What you need:

Glass

Salt

¾ glass water

¼ cup vegetable oil

12 drops food colouring

What to do:

Step 1. Add food colouring and vegetable oil to the glass of water.

Step 2. Sprinkle salt on top of the oil.

Step 3. Watch the lava blobs move up and down in your glass!

💡 **What just happened?** The oil floats on top of the water because it is lighter than the water. The salt sinks down to the water, taking some oil with it. Once the salt dissolves, the oil goes back up.

134. Motion Ocean

Duration of Experiment: 15 mins.   Difficulty Level: ▬ ▬ ▬

What you need:

| Jar | Water | 10 drops food colouring | Glitter | Baby oil | Plastic floating toys |

What to do:

Step 1. Fill half the jar with water. Add the food colouring and glitter.

Step 2. Add baby oil till $\frac{3^{th}}{4}$ of the jar is full.

Step 3. Place a floating toy on top of the oil. Screw the lid on.

Step 4. Shake the jar gently to set your ocean in motion.

💡 **What just happened?** Water is denser than oil. The two liquids never mix. When the water moves, it pushes the oil around, making shapes like waves.

135. Cool Crystals

Duration of Experiment: 7-8 days   Difficulty Level: ▬ ▬ ▬

What you need:

| Jars | Paper clips | Woollen thread | Baking soda | Dish | Spoon | Hot water |

What to do:

Step 1. Fill two jars with hot water.

Step 2. Add baking soda until you can't dissolve any more.

Step 3. Attach paper clip to the ends of the thread.

Step 4. Suspend it in the jars, as shown.

Step 5. Place a dish under the lowest part of the thread. Crystals form in a week.

💡 **What just happened?** The baking soda drips off the lowest point of the thread onto the plate. However, a small amount of the baking soda remains on the thread after each drip.

136. Crazy Lava Lamp

Duration of Experiment: ⏱ **30** mins.   Difficulty Level: ▬▬ ▬▬ ▬▬

What you need:

Antacid tablet

Plastic bottle

Vegetable oil

12 drops food colouring

Water

What to do:

Step 1. Fill $\frac{1}{4}^{th}$ of the bottle with water and $\frac{1}{4}^{th}$ with oil.

Step 2. Wait until the oil and water have separated. Add the food colouring to the bottle.

Step 3. Cut the antacid tablet into 5 pieces and drop one of them into the bottle.

Step 4. You should soon be able to see coloured bubbles floating to the top, just like in a real lava lamp.

Step 5. You can even shine a flashlight through the bottom of the bottle to make it look cooler.

SCIENCE AROUND US

Lava Lamps

Actual lava lamps contain wax in a clear liquid. The melted wax rises as it gets heated by the bulb at the bottom and falls as it cools. But the basic principle behind your lamp and the fancy ones is exactly the same!

💡 **What just happened?** The oil settled on top of the water because of its lower density. The food colouring mixed with the water at the bottom. The piece of antacid tablet released small bubbles of carbon dioxide gas that rose to the top and took some of the coloured water along for the ride.

137. Floating Cans

Duration of Experiment: 5 mins.   Difficulty Level: ▬▬▭▭

What you need:

Cola can   Diet Cola can   Water   Bowl

What to do:

Step 1. Check to make sure that the weight of both the cans is equal.

Step 2. Fill the bowl with water. Put both the cans in the bowl. Do you think they will float or sink?

💡 **What just happened?** Contrary to what you thought, the regular cola can sinks, while the diet cola can floats. Regular cola contains a greater quantity of sweetener than diet cola. This makes its density greater than water, causing it to sink.

138. Rainbow in a Glass

Duration of Experiment: 30 mins.   Difficulty Level: ▬▬▭

What you need:

Honey   Dishwashing liquid   Water   Vegetable oil   Rubbing alcohol   Tall glass   Blue food colouring

What to do:

Step 1. Fill $\frac{1}{4}^{th}$ of the glass with honey.

Step 2. Tip the glass slightly and add dishwashing liquid.

Step 3. Mix some food colouring and water and add it to the glass.

Step 4. Add some vegetable oil to the mixture.

Step 5. Finally, add the rubbing alcohol.

💡 **What just happened?** Denser liquids settle at the bottom, while the less dense liquids float to the top.

139. Magic Corn

Duration of Experiment: ⏱ 15 mins.   Difficulty Level: ▬ ▬ ▬

What you need:

Un-popped corn

Ball bearing

Ping pong ball

Jar

What to do:

Step 1. Put the ping pong ball in the jar and fill it with corn.

Step 2. Put the ball bearing on top. Swirl it around.

Step 3. The ball bearing will sink to the bottom and the ping pong ball will come to the surface.

💡 **What just happened?** Since the ball bearing has a greater density, it sinks down and the ping-pong ball finds its way up.

140. Water Exchange

Duration of Experiment: ⏱ 10 mins.   Difficulty Level: ▬ ▬ ▬

What you need:

Jars

Hot water and cold water

Cardboard

Red and blue food colouring

What to do:

Step 1. Fill one jar with hot water. Add blue food colouring.

Step 2. Fill the other jar with cold water. Add red food colouring.

Step 3. Cover the red jar with the cardboard.

Step 4. Turn the red jar over the blue jar and take the cardboard piece out.

Step 5. The blue water will move up and the red water will move down.

💡 **What just happened?** Hot water has a lower density than cold water, which means that it is lighter. So, the cold water sinks to the bottom and the hot water makes its way up.

141. Bottle Accelerometer

Duration of Experiment: 10 mins.   Difficulty Level:

What you need:

Cork   String   Thumb tack   2 l plastic bottle   Water

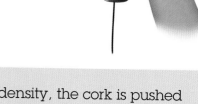

What to do:

Step 1. Attach one end of the string to the cork with the thumb tack.

Step 2. Put this in the bottle of water and screw the cap over the other end of the string.

Step 3. Turn the bottle over and walk around the room.

The cork moves in whichever direction you move!

What just happened? Because water has a greater density, the cork is pushed forward when you walk.

142. Hot Stuff

Duration of Experiment: 15 mins.   Difficulty Level:

What you need:

Small glass bottle   Glass bowl   Red food colouring   String   Hot water   Cold water

What to do:

Step 1. Pour cold water in the glass bowl.

Step 2. Fill the small glass bottle with hot water.
Add red food colouring.

Step 3. Slowly suspend this small bottle into the glass bowl with the help of the string.

Step 4. You will notice the red water rising from the bottle.

What just happened? Hot water rises because the density of hot water is less than that of cold water, making it lighter. Hence, the red coloured hot water rises and settles above the cold water.

143. Salty Straws

Duration of Experiment: ⏱ 15 mins.   Difficulty Level:

What you need:

| Six cups | Salt | Food colouring | Straw | Water |

What to do:

Step 1. Add 1 teaspoon of salt to the first cup, two to the second and so on.

Step 2. Put a different food colouring in each cup.

Step 3. Dip the straw into the first cup.

Step 4. Block the other end of the straw and take it out.

Step 5. Dip it into the second cup and release it.

Step 6. Once water enters the straw, block it again. Repeat steps 4 and 5 for all cups.

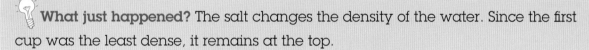

💡 **What just happened?** The salt changes the density of the water. Since the first cup was the least dense, it remains at the top.

144. Rock Candy

Duration of Experiment: ⏱ 7 days   Difficulty Level:

What you need:

| Food colouring | Pan | Water | 2 cups of sugar | Jar | Wooden chopstick | Spoon |

What to do:

Step 1. Put the water, food colouring and sugar in the pan.

Step 2. Bring it to a boil and keep stirring till all the sugar has dissolved.

Step 3. Pour this syrup into the jar and put the wooden chopsticks in it.

Step 4. Leave it untouched for a week. Enjoy your rock candy after that.

💡 **What just happened?** The hot water was saturated with sugar. As it cooled, it could not retain the sugar, which crystallised on the chopsticks.

145. Gummy Bear Expansion

Duration of Experiment: **24** hours   Difficulty Level: ▬ ▬ ▬

What you need:

Gummy bears   Bowl   Water

What to do:

Step 1. Fill half the bowl with water.

Step 2. Put one gummy bear in it.

Step 3. Leave it overnight.

Step 4. It will become twice its size by the next morning!

💡 **What just happened?** Water always flows from areas of lower density to higher density. Gummy bears are very dense, making it easy for them to absorb the water-like a sponge.

146. Three Layered Float

Duration of Experiment: **30** mins.   Difficulty Level: ▬ ▬ ▬

What you need:

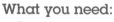 

Oil   Cork   Coin   Water   Honey   Grapes   Tall glass   Raisins

What to do:

Step 1. Fill $\frac{1}{3}^{rd}$ of the glass with honey, $\frac{1}{3}^{rd}$ with oil and the rest with water.

Step 2. Once the substances have settled, drop in the raisin, grapes, cork and coin into the glass.

Step 3. The cork floats on top, the coin sinks to the bottom, but the raisins remain suspended in the middle!

💡 **What just happened?** All three items (raisins, coin and cork) have different densities and float in separate layers according to their density.

147. Floating Golf Ball

Duration of Experiment: ⏱ 15 mins.   Difficulty Level: ▬ ▬ ▬

What you need:

Golf ball   Salt   Plastic container   Water

What to do:

Step 1. Fill half the container with water.

Step 2. Dissolve salt in the container till you can dissolve no more.

Step 3. Place the golf ball on the water. It should float.

Step 4. Add more fresh water. The ball remains suspended in the middle of the jar!

💡 **What just happened?** The salt water is denser than the golf ball. So, it floats. However, the fresh water is less dense than the ball, which is why it remains suspended.

148. Oily Ice

Duration of Experiment: ⏱ 30 mins.   Difficulty Level: ▬ ▬ ▬

What you need:

Food colouring   Vegetable oil   Baby oil   Ice cubes   Glass

What to do:

Step 1. Add two drops of food colouring to an empty glass.

Step 2. Fill half the glass with vegetable oil and the rest with baby oil.

Step 3. Drop an ice cube in it. It settles in the middle of the glass.

Step 4. After 10 minutes, you will be able to see a drop begin to melt away from the ice cube.

Step 5. It settles down in slow motion and mixes with the food colouring.

💡 **What just happened?** The baby oil settles on top of the vegetable oil because it is low in density. The ice settles in the middle because it is more dense than the baby oil, but lesser than vegetable oil. However, water is more dense than ice and sinks to the bottom.

149. Colourful Crystals!

Duration of Experiment: ⏱ **40** hours   Difficulty Level: ▬ ▬▬ ▬▬

What you need:

Eggshells   Glue   Alum powder   Spoon   Water   Measuring cup   Food colouring

What to do:

Step 1. Crack your eggshell into two.

Step 2. Spread a thin layer of glue on the inside.

Step 3. While the glue is still wet, sprinkle it with alum powder. Leave the eggshells in the box to dry overnight.

Step 4. The next day, add five drops of food colouring to about two cups of water.

Step 5. Heat the water till it is almost boiling.

Step 6. Pour $\frac{3}{4}^{th}$ cup of alum powder into the water and stir it till all the alum is dissolved. Drop the eggshell into this mixture and let it cool overnight.

Step 7. Pick them up the next morning and enjoy your pretty coloured crystals!

💡 **What just happened?** When the water is hot, it is less dense than cold water. Hence, you are able to dissolve more alum powder in the hot water.

When the water starts cooling, it becomes denser and there is no space for the alum. So it crystallises in the egg.

150. Magic Rice

Duration of Experiment: ⏱ **10** mins.   Difficulty Level: ▬ ▬ ▬

What you need:

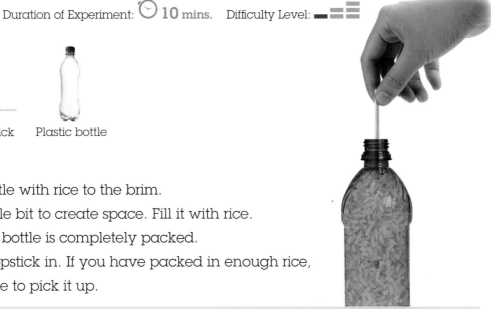

Rice   Chopstick   Plastic bottle

What to do:

Step 1. Fill the bottle with rice to the brim.

Step 2. Tap it a little bit to create space. Fill it with rice.
Repeat this till the bottle is completely packed.

Step 3. Stick a chopstick in. If you have packed in enough rice,
you should be able to pick it up.

💡 **What just happened?** The bottle is very densely packed with rice. The rice has very little space to move, so the chopstick gets wedged between the rice and the sides of the bottle.

151. Drinkable Density

Duration of Experiment: ⏱ **10** mins.   Difficulty Level: ▬ ▬ ▬

What you need:

Pomegranate juice Orange juice White grape juice Eye dropper Glass

What to do:

Step 1. Pour the white grape juice in the glass.

Step 2. Use the eye dropper to drop the orange juice on top of it.

Step 3. Finally, drop the pomegranate juice on top.

💡 **What just happened?** The juices are of different densities because of the differing amounts of sugar dissolved in them. White grape juice has the most sugar and pomegranate juice the least.

LET THERE BE LIGHT

Experiments on the principle of light

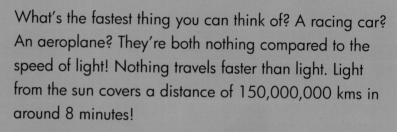

What's the fastest thing you can think of? A racing car? An aeroplane? They're both nothing compared to the speed of light! Nothing travels faster than light. Light from the sun covers a distance of 150,000,000 kms in around 8 minutes!

In fact, it has been hypothesised that if we could find a way to travel faster than the speed of light, time travel may actually be possible. Sounds cool, doesn't it?

152. Make a Rainbow

Duration of Experiment: ⏱ 10 mins.   Difficulty Level: ▬ ▬ ▬

What you need:

Glass   Water   White paper

What to do:

Step 1. Fill three quarters of the glass with water.

Step 2. Take the glass and the paper to your window.

Step 3. Hold the glass above the paper. Let sunlight pass through the glass and fall on the paper.

Step 4. Adjust your paper a little till you see a mini rainbow on it.

 What just happened? When sunlight passes through water, it refracts or bends, splitting into seven colours. This is what you just created on your paper.

153. Make Your Own Kaleidoscope

Duration of Experiment: ⏱ **20 mins.** Difficulty Level: ▬▬ ▬▬ ▬▬

What you need:

Tape   Ruler   Glass cutter   Sequins   Cardboard   Mirror

What to do:

Step 1. Cut the mirror into three 4 × 15 cm strips using the glass cutter.

Step 2. Cut the cardboard into three similar strips.

Step 3. Paste the cardboard strips on the back of the mirror. Tape the three strips together in the form of a triangle.

Step 4. Look at some sequins through the kaleidoscope and rotate it. Enjoy the colourful display.

💡 **What just happened?** Light travels in a straight line. But when it hits the mirror, it is reflected. The reflections bounce back and forth from side to side, creating multiple images.

154. Water Magnifier

Duration of Experiment: ⏱ **5 mins.** Difficulty Level: ▬▬ ▬▬ ▬▬

What you need:

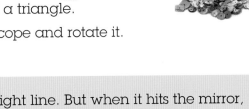

Eye dropper   Transparent plastic square   Water

What to do:

Step 1. Place the plastic square on a page of fine print.

Step 2. Add a drop of water to the centre of the plastic.

Step 3. Watch how the print under the water is magnified.

💡 **What just happened?** The water acts as a lens. The lens bends the light from the image underneath it to your eye, making the image appear larger.

155. Reading Light

Duration of Experiment: 15 mins.   Difficulty Level:

What you need:

Tape   Scissors   Aluminium foil   Paraffin wax blocks

What to do:

Step 1. Cut a piece of aluminium foil in the same size as the two wax blocks.

Step 2. Tape the foil between the two blocks.

Step 3. Your photometer is ready. If the top block is brighter, the top half of the room is brighter than the bottom half.

What just happened? Wax is a translucent material. The light can enter it and is reflected back through the block by the aluminium foil. Thus, you can measure light intensity by the brightness of the block.

156. Sundial

Duration of Experiment: 12 hours   Difficulty Level:

What you need:

Stick   Watch

What to do:

Step 1. Fix the stick vertically into the ground.

Step 2. Every hour, mark where the shadow of the stick is falling. Number the marking depending on the time.

Step 3. To see the time, just look at the shadow and read the corresponding number.

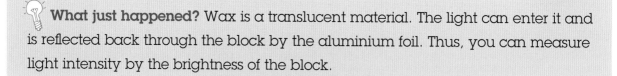

What just happened? The shadow of the stick depends upon the position of the Sun, which changes every hour.

157. Mirror Mirror

Duration of Experiment: ⏱ 10 mins.   Difficulty Level: ▬▬▬

What you need:

Comb   Torch   Cardboard   Black paper   Hand mirror   Masking tape   Scissors

What to do:

Step 1. Cut a small hole in the middle of the cardboard.

Step 2. Tape a comb across the hole.

Step 3. Place the cardboard vertically on the black paper.

Step 4. Go to a dark room. Shine the torch through the comb.

Step 5. Hold a mirror in front of the light.

Step 6. Change the angle of the mirror and watch the direction of the light change!

💡 **What just happened?** Light travels in the same direction till it hits an object. On hitting a mirror, it is reflected back at the same angle as the one it hit the mirror with.

158. Vanishing Coin

Duration of Experiment: ⏱ 5 mins.   Difficulty Level: ▬▬▬

What you need:

Coin   Glass   Water

What to do:

Step 1. Put the coin on the table.

Step 2. Put the glass on top of the coin.

Step 3. Fill the glass with water and watch as the coin disappears from your sight!

💡 **What just happened?** Glass and water causes light to 'bend'. Therefore, the coin can't be seen once you pour water into the glass.

159. Double the Money

Duration of Experiment: 5 mins.   Difficulty Level: ▬ ▤ ▤

What you need:

Coin   Bowl   Water

What to do:

Step 1. Drop the coin into the empty bowl.

Step 2. Slowly pour water into the bowl.

Step 3. At one point of time, you should be able to see two coins in the bowl instead of just one.

💡 **What just happened?** The water causes the light to 'bend' and hence you can see two coins instead of one.

160. Make White Light

Duration of Experiment: 🕐 15 mins.   Difficulty Level: ▤ ▬ ▤

What you need:

Rubber band   3 torches   Red, blue and green   White paper
                                 cellophane paper

What to do:

Step 1. Stretch a different coloured paper over each torch. Secure them with rubber bands.

Step 2. Shine all three torches on the paper simultaneously.

Step 3. Adjust the distance between each torch and the paper.

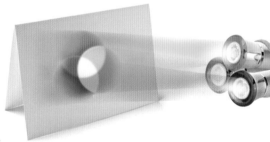

Step 4. You will see a spot on the paper where all three lights mix to form white light.

💡 **What just happened?** When red, green and blue light mix, they form a kind of light that is very similar to white light. Our eyes perceive this as white itself.

161. Let There be Light

Duration of Experiment: ⏱ 20 mins.   Difficulty Level: ▬▬ ▬▬ ▬▬

What you need:

Liquid soap

Torch

White card paper

Wet glass

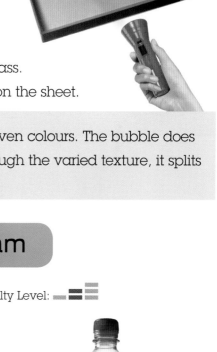

What to do:

Step 1. Put the glass on top of a table. Keep the white paper about 10 cm behind this.

Step 2. Place the torch 75 cm in front of the glass.

Step 3. Blow a liquid soap bubble and place it on the glass.

Step 4. Switch the torch on. You will see coloured bands on the sheet.

💡 **What just happened?** White light is made up of seven colours. The bubble does not have uniform thickness. When the light passes through the varied texture, it splits into different colours.

162. Bottled Beam

Duration of Experiment: ⏱ 10 mins.   Difficulty Level: ▬▬ ▬▬ ▬▬

What you need:

Torch

Bottle

Water

Nails

What to do:

Step 1. Make a hole in the side of the bottle near the base.

Step 2. Cover the hole with your finger. Fill the bottle with water.

Step 3. Shine a torch through the other side of the bottle.

Step 4. Move your hand down the stream of water. You should be able to see a spot of light on your hand.

💡 **What just happened?** In this case, light does not travel in a straight line and 'bends' to reach your hand. Water acts like a mirror, reflecting light within its stream.

163. Make an Eclipse

Duration of Experiment: 10 mins.   Difficulty Level:

What you need:

String   Ping-pong ball   Lamp   Globe   Tape

What to do:

Step 1. Attach a piece of string to the ping-pong ball with the tape.

Step 2. Switch on the lamp. Suspend the ball between the lamp and the globe.

Step 3. Notice how the shadow forms on the globe.

💡 **What just happened?** The lamp represents the Sun, the ball is the moon and the globe is the Earth. An actual solar eclipse takes place in the same way when the moon comes in between the Sun and the Earth.

164. Calculate the Speed of Light

Duration of Experiment: 5 mins.   Difficulty Level:

What you need:

Chocolate bar   Microwave

What to do:

Step 1. Turn off the rotation function in the microwave.

Step 2. Place the chocolate lengthwise in the microwave.

Step 3. Turn the microwave on and stop it when you can see the surface of the chocolate melting slightly.

Step 4. Find the two softest points on the chocolate and measure the distance between them.

Step 5. Multiply this distance by two. Then, multiply that by the frequency of the microwave. Voila! That's the speed of light!

💡 **What just happened?** The waves from a microwave travel at the same speed as the light. Multiplying its wavelength and its frequency gives us the speed of light.

165. Hot Hot!

Duration of Experiment: ⏱ 30 mins.   Difficulty Level: ▬ ▬ ▬

What you need:

Magnifying glass   Paper

What to do:

Step 1. Go to a sunny area.

Step 2. Hold the magnifying glass above the paper such that all the sunlight is concentrated on one point.

Step 3. Hold it there for a while and you will soon burn a hole in the paper.

💡 **What just happened?** The magnifying glass concentrates all the heat and light from the Sun on that one point. This generates enough heat to burn the paper.

166. Make a Periscope

Duration of Experiment: ⏱ 60 mins.   Difficulty Level: ▬ ▬ ▬

What you need:

Glue   Paper cutter   Mirrors   Shoe box   Tape

What to do:

Step 1. Cut two holes on opposite sides of the shoe box, leaving space from the ends.

Step 2. Paste the two mirrors at a 45° angle inside the box on either sides.

Step 3. Look through the bottom rectangle and keep adjusting both the mirrors till you can see what is outside the rectangle on top. Stick the mirrors using the glue and tape.

Step 4. Cover the box with the lid and seal it with the tape.

💡 **What just happened?** Light hits the mirror through the top window and gets reflected. It travels straight down and hits the lower mirror, which reflects the light straight to your eye.

167. Coloured Light

Duration of Experiment: ⏱ **30** mins.   Difficulty Level: ▬ ▬ ▬

What you need:

CD

Scissors

Aluminium foil

Cereal box

Scotch tape

Pencil

Protractor

Ruler

What to do:

Step 1. Measure 1.5 inches from one end of the box and make a mark on the top of it along its length.

Step 2. Draw a straight line across the width of the box from this mark.

Step 3. Cut along this line. Cut off the flaps you just created.

Step 4. From the edge of the box that you just cut, draw a 3-inch line at a 45° angle with a protractor. Cut a similar slit on the other side of the box. Place the CD in this slit.

Step 5. On the opposite side of the box, cut a rectangle with a 1-inch height, half an inch from the top of the box.

Step 6. Cover half the rectangle with a piece of aluminium. Leave a gap of 1 mm and cover the other half of the rectangle with another piece of foil.

Step 7. Tape the box shut. Point the slit at a light source and look at it through the square hole.

Step 8. You will be able to see individual colours of the light!

💡 **What just happened?** Light enters the spectrometer through the thin slit. Since the slit is so thin, the light splits into its seven component colours when it hits the CD. These are the seven colours you see when you look through the square.

168. Telescope

Duration of Experiment: ⏱ **60** mins.   Difficulty Level: ▬ ▬ ▬

What you need:

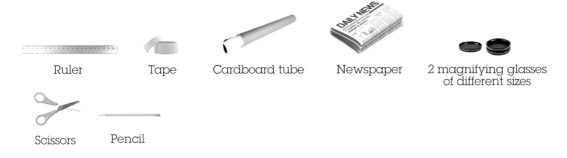

Ruler   Tape   Cardboard tube   Newspaper   2 magnifying glasses
of different sizes

Scissors   Pencil

What to do:

Step 1. Hold the larger magnifying glass between yourself and the paper. The print will look blurry.

Step 2. Hold the second magnifying glass between your eye and the first magnifying glass.
Adjust it till the print is sharp.

Step 3. Measure the distance between the two magnifying glasses and write it down.

Step 4. Cut a slot in the cardboard tube near the front. The slot should be able to hold the magnifying glass.

Step 5. Measure the distance you had written earlier and cut a slot at that distance from the first slot.

Step 6. Tape both the glasses in the slots – the larger one in front and the smaller one closer to the eye.

Step 7. Look through the end to use your telescope!

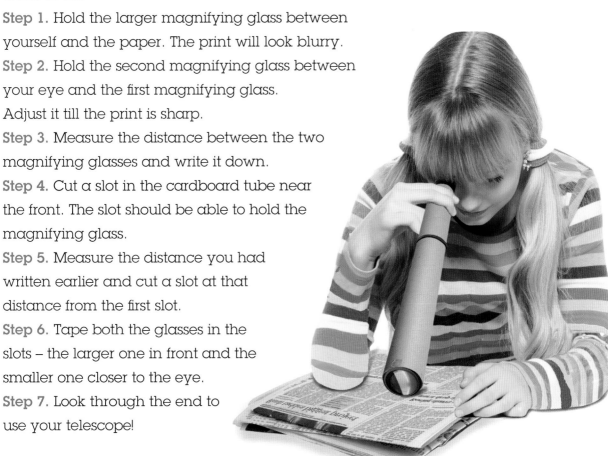

💡 **What just happened?** The larger glass collects light from a distance. The smaller lens magnifies this image.

169. Bend Light

Duration of Experiment: 10 mins.   Difficulty Level:

What you need:

Scissors   Shoe box   Torch   Jar   Water

What to do:

Step 1. Cut a small slit in one end of the shoe box.

Step 2. Fill the jar with water.

Step 3. Put the jar in the box against the slit.

Step 4. Go to a dark room and shine a torch through the slit.

Step 5. Watch the light 'bend'!

What just happened? Light 'bends' or refracts because of the different speeds of light in air and water. When light enters water, it bends and does so once again while exiting.

170. Magnify it

Duration of Experiment: 10 mins.   Difficulty Level:

What you need:

Tape   Scissors   Needle   Aluminium foil   White cardboard

What to do:

Step 1. Cut out a 30 × 30 mm square in the cardboard.

Step 2. Cover it with aluminium foil using the tape.

Step 3. Make a tiny hole in the middle of the foil with the needle.

Step 4. Look at small print through the hole and notice how it looks bigger now.

What just happened? When you use the pinhole, the rays from the object enter the eye through the pinhole at a larger angle, forming a larger image on the retina.

171. Bending Light

Duration of Experiment: 🕐 **10** mins. Difficulty Level:

What you need:

| Pencil | Ruler | Glass slab | Paper |

What to do:

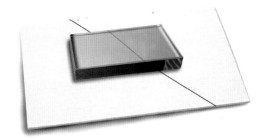

Step 1. Put the glass slab on the paper and trace it.

Step 2. Remove the glass slab and draw a slanting line till one edge of the slab.

Step 3. Place the slab back. Look through the other edge and continue the line.

Step 4. Lift the slab. You can see how much a ray of light bends through glass.

💡 **What just happened?** Light travels at different speeds through air and glass. The change in speed also causes a change in the direction.

172. Newton's Colour Disc

Duration of Experiment: 🕐 **30** mins. Difficulty Level:

What you need:

| Felt pens | Nail | Pencil | Cardboard | Glue | Paper |

What to do:

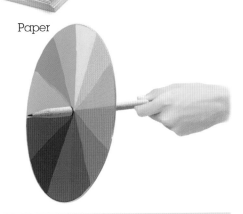

Step 1. Use your felt pens on paper to make the disc shown or print it out from the Internet.

Step 2. Glue it onto the cardboard and allow it to dry.

Step 3. Use the nail to make a hole in the centre.

Step 4. Put a pencil in the hole and spin it.

Step 5. The disc should look entirely white.

💡 **What just happened?** White light is made up of all these colours in different wavelengths. Spinning the disc mixes all the wavelengths and it looks white.

173. Black Tomato

Duration of Experiment: ⏱ **10** mins.   Difficulty Level: ▬▬ ▬▬ ▬▬

What you need:

Torch   Rubber band   Red tomato   Green cellophane paper

What to do:

Step 1. Cover the torch with the green cellophane.

Step 2. Go into a dark room. Shine the 'green torch' on the tomato.

Step 3. The tomato will look black.

💡 **What just happened?** The colour you see depends on which colour is reflected by that object. A tomato is red because it absorbs all the colours, except red. In green light, there is no red to reflect. Hence, the tomato looks black.

174. Light Jelly

Duration of Experiment: ⏱ **24** hours   Difficulty Level: ▬▬ ▬▬ ▬▬

What you need:

Torch   Bowl   Water   2 packets jelly powder   Box   Knife   Cutting board

What to do:

Step 1. Mix the water and the jelly in the bowl and bring it to a boil.

Step 2. Pour the jelly into the box and let it set in the fridge overnight.

Step 3. Take the jelly out onto a board.

Step 4. Use the knife to cut the jelly into different lens shapes.

Step 5. Shine the torch through these 'lenses' and see how the light bends.

💡 **What just happened?** The jelly acts just like a lens. If you cut it in the shape of a concave lens, the light is likely to spread out. If you cut it in the shape of a convex lens, the light is likely to come together.

175. Make a Pinhole Camera

Duration of Experiment: 60 mins.   Difficulty Level: ▬ ▬ ▬

What you need:

Shoebox

Aluminium foil

Tape

Scissors

Needle

Tracing paper

What to do:

Step 1. Cut out two rectangles on opposite sides of the shoe box.

Step 2. Cover one rectangle with the foil and make a small hole in it with the needle.

Step 3. Cover the other rectangle with the tracing paper.

Step 4. Tape the lid of the shoe box on.

Step 5. Point the pinhole towards a bright object (like your window). You should be able to see whatever is outside the window upside down on the tracing paper!

SCIENCE AROUND US

How do cameras work?

A film camera is very similar to the pinhole camera you just made. There is a film strip coated with a substance that is very sensitive to light in place of the tracing paper. Light enters the camera through the shutter (like the pinhole), which opens for a split second. The light falls on the film strip, which captures the image.

What just happened? Light travels in a straight line. Hence, light from the top of the image travels in a straight line to the screen, as does the light from the bottom. However, they cross over because of the pinhole, creating an upside down image.

176. Twinkle Twinkle Little Star

Duration of Experiment: ⏱ 30 mins.   Difficulty Level: ▬▬ ▬▬ ▬▬

What you need:

Bowl   Water   Aluminium foil   Torch   Black paint   Pins   Paint brush

Marbles   Scissors   Blanket

What to do:

Step 1. Cut a circle in the centre of the foil that is as big as the mouth of the torch.

Step 2. Wrap the insides of the bowl with foil with the shiny side facing inwards and the hole facing the bottom

Step 3. Fill $\frac{3}{4}^{th}$ of the bowl with water.

Step 4. Put a few marbles in the bowl.

Step 5. Cover the top of the bowl with foil, shiny side facing inwards.

Step 6. Paint the top of this foil black.

Step 7. Make a few holes in the foil with the pins.

Step 8. Cover your head with a thick blanket and shine the torchlight through the bottom of the bowl, where the hole was made. Look at the bowl from the top. You will be able to see 'twinkling stars'.

💡 **What just happened?** The light from the torch is reflected by the foil and bounces all over the bowl. However, the marbles come in the way, casting shadows. But as the water moves, the light bends, sometimes reaching your eye and sometimes not. This is exactly how stars twinkle in reality. As the light travels through the different layers of the atmosphere, the light from the stars bend.

SOUND EFFECTS

Experiments on the principle of sound

Try to imagine a world without sound. You wouldn't be able to listen to music, watch TV or even talk to anyone!

Sound travels in waves and needs a medium to travel. Hence, sound can travel through liquids like water, gases like air and solids like wood. Did you know that in space, where there is a vacuum (no air), astronauts cannot speak to each other the way we do? They use walkie talkies and ear pieces to talk to each other when they are not in their capsule!

177. Musical Glasses

Duration of Experiment: 20 mins.   Difficulty Level:

What you need:

Glasses   Pencil   Water

What to do:

Step 1. Put all the glasses in a line. Fill the first one with a little water, the second with slightly more and so on.

Step 2. Hit the glass with the least amount of water using a pencil and observe the sound. Then, hit the glass with the most water. Notice the difference in the sound.

Step 3. Enjoy creating a tune!

💡 **What just happened?** Small vibrations are made when you hit the glass; this creates sound waves which travel through the water. More water means slower vibrations and a deeper tone.

178. Duck Calls

 Duration of Experiment: ⏱ 10 mins.   Difficulty Level: ▬ ▬ ▬

What you need:

Straw   Scissors

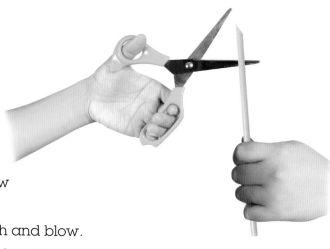

What to do:

Step 1. Flatten one end of the straw.

Step 2. Cut the flattened end of the straw
in the shape of a pointy 'V'.

Step 3. Put the pointy end in your mouth and blow.

Step 4. You can hear a sound like a duck call!

💡 **What just happened?** The flaps of the pointy end vibrate very fast against each other when you blow through the straw. These vibrations create the noise.

179. Straw Flute

Duration of Experiment: ⏱ 10 mins.   Difficulty Level: ▬ ▬ ▬

What you need:

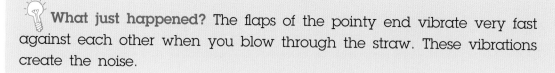

Straw   Scissors

What to do:

Step 1. Flatten one end of the straw.

Step 2. Cut the flattened end of the straw into a pointy 'V'.

Step 3. Cut three holes in the straw along the length of the straw.

Step 4. Put the pointy end in your mouth and blow.

Step 5. Close each of the holes and blow. See how the sound differs!

💡 **What just happened?** When you blow into the straw, it causes a vibration. The pitch of the sound depends on the time taken by the vibration to travel from one hole to the other. That is why, when you block different holes, the vibration travels different distances, making you hear different sounds!

180. The Clucking Cup

Duration of Experiment: 🕐 15 mins.   Difficulty Level: ▬▬ ▬▬

What you need:

Plastic cup

String

Paper clip

Paper towel

Scissors

Water

What to do:

Step 1. Make a hole in the centre of the base of the cup.

Step 2. Tie one end of the string to the middle of the paper clip.

Step 3. Push the other end of the string through the hole in the cup.

Step 4. Hold the cup upside down in one hand.

Step 5. Wet a paper towel and fold it.

Step 6. Wrap the paper towel around the string and tug on it in short jerks.

Step 7. The sound you create is a lot like a clucking hen!

What causes echoes?

An echo occurs when a sound wave bounces off a surface and arrives at the listener some time after the direct sound. Echoes can be very useful in finding out the depth of the ocean and finding things lost at sea.

SCIENCE AROUND US

💡 **What just happened?** Tugging on the string makes it vibrate, creating a sound. The shape of the cup amplifies this sound, giving rise to the fascinating sound.

181. Jumping Rice

Duration of Experiment: 10 mins.   Difficulty Level: ▬ ▬ ▬

What you need:

Rice   Bowl   Pan   Spoon   Cling wrap   Rubber bands

What to do:

Step 1. Stretch the cling wrap over the top of the bowl and secure it with a rubber band.

Step 2. Sprinkle a few grains of rice on top.

Step 3. Hold the pan close and hit it with the spoon to see the rice jump!

💡 **What just happened?** Sound travels in the form of waves. The waves travel through the air and hit the cling wrap, making it vibrate. The vibrations cause the rice to jump.

182. Screeching Cellophane

Duration of Experiment: ⏱ 5 mins.   Difficulty Level: ▬ ▬ ▬

What you need:

Cellophane paper

What to do:

Step 1. Hold the cellophane tightly between your thumbs and index fingers. Hold it just below your lips.

Step 2. Keep your lips close together. Blow straight at the edge of the cellophane.

Step 3. Adjust the distance between your mouth and the cellophane paper till you hear a high pitch screech.

💡 **What just happened?** The fast moving air from your lips makes the edge of the cellophane vibrate very fast. This creates a high tone.

183. The Spoon Bell

Duration of Experiment: 5 mins.   Difficulty Level:

What you need:

| Scissors | String | Metal spoon | Table |

What to do:

Step 1. Tie the spoon in the middle of the string.

Step 2. Hold one end of the thread to your right ear and the other to your left ear.

Step 3. Walk to the table and swing slowly so that the spoon gently bangs against the edge of the table. It will sound like a bell.

💡 **What just happened?** The metal begins to vibrate when you bang it against the table. These vibrations are carried by the strings straight up to your ears.

184. Sound in a Jar

Duration of Experiment: 🕐 5 mins.   Difficulty Level:

What you need:

| Straw | Clay | Screwdriver | Airtight jar | Buzzer or any small object that creates a continuous sound |

What to do:

Step 1. Use the screwdriver to make a hole in the lid of the jar.

Step 2. Set the buzzer off and put it in the jar.

Step 3. Put the straw through the hole in the lid and seal it in place with the clay.

Step 4. Suck all the air out of the jar through the straw. Pinch the straw between breaths to make sure no air escapes.

Step 5. The sound from the buzzer slowly disappears.

💡 **What just happened?** Sound needs a medium to travel. There is no sound in a vacuum. Once you sucked all the air out of the jar, you couldn't hear the buzzer.

185. Bottle Organ

Duration of Experiment: ⏱ **30** mins.   Difficulty Level:

What you need:

Glass bottles   Water

What to do:

Step 1. Put the glass bottles in a row.

Step 2. Fill water in each bottle. There should be a little more water in each successive bottle.

Step 3. Blow across the mouth of each bottle. You should hear notes of different kinds.

Step 4. If you get tired of blowing, you can simply take a wooden ruler and hit each bottle to make a kind of xylophone!

💡 **What just happened?** By blowing a strong jet of air across the mouth of the bottle, some amount of air is going into it. Once it gets full, there is nowhere for it to escape. The pressure builds up till the jet is pushed out of the bottle. This causes a vibration. When there is more water in the bottle, there is less space. So the vibrations are shorter and the pitch is higher.

186. Hello!

Duration of Experiment: ⏱ **10** mins.   Difficulty Level: ▬ ▬▬ ▬▬

What you need:

String   2 tin cans   Scissors

What to do:

Step 1. Cut a long piece of string (around 6 feet).

Step 2. Make a small hole at the bottom of both cans.

Step 3. Thread the string through each can and tie a knot to secure it.

Step 4. Ask a friend to take one can and stand at a distance that makes the string completely tight.

Step 5. Hold your can to your ear.

Step 6. Ask your friend to talk into hers. Then, exchange places and talk into the can and ask your friend to listen.

💡 **What just happened?** Speaking into the can creates sound waves that are converted into vibrations at the bottom of the can. These vibrations travel along the string and are converted back into sound waves.

187. Roaring Balloon

Duration of Experiment: ⏱ 5 mins.   Difficulty Level: ▬ ▬ ▬

What you need:

Coins   Balloon

What to do:

Step 1. Put a rough edged coin into the empty balloon and blow it up.

Step 2. Swirl the balloon around such that the coin is rolling against the balloon.

Step 3. You should be able to hear your balloon roar!

💡 **What just happened?** The edge of the coin is rough and bounces on the balloon's surface. This causes small vibrations. The noise is magnified by the air in the balloon.

188. Sounds of Ruler

Duration of Experiment: ⏱ 5 mins.   Difficulty Level: ▬ ▬ ▬

What you need:

Steel ruler   Wooden
                    board

What to do:

Step 1. Press one end of the ruler down on the board, letting the other end protrude over the edge.

Step 2. Push the free end down and let it go.

Step 3. As it vibrates, you will be able to hear a low pitched sound.

💡 **What just happened?** All sound is made by vibrations. When you release the ruler, it vibrates, making the noise. The faster the vibrations, the higher the pitch will be.

189. Strum Away

Duration of Experiment: 15 mins.   Difficulty Level:

What you need:

Rubber bands   Cardboard box

What to do:

Step 1. Stretch the rubber bands over the cardboard box.

Step 2. Pull one rubber band and let it go. Notice the sound.

Step 3. Pull the rubber band a little more and let it go. Notice the difference in sound.

What just happened? In the first case, the rubber band only vibrated through a very short distance, making a weak sound. In the second case, the vibrations were stronger and so was the sound.

190. Music Box

Duration of Experiment: 30 mins.   Difficulty Level:

What you need:

Large matchbox   Rubber bands   Cardboard   Glue   Scissors

What to do:

Step 1. Cut a right angled triangle out of the cardboard. The length of the base should be the same as the width of the matchbox.

Step 2. Make four grooves along the hypotenuse.

Step 3. Stick the right angled triangle across the middle of the matchbox.

Step 4. Stretch the rubber bands over the matchbox. Let the rubber bands rest in the grooves.

Step 5. Pluck each rubber band. Each one will give a different sound.

What just happened? The different sounds are produced by different vibrations. The more the rubber band is stretched, the higher the pitch will be.

191. Nail Piano

Duration of Experiment: 🕐 30 mins.   Difficulty Level: ▬▬ ═ ▆

What you need:

Nails   Hammer   Plank of wood   Small block of wood

What to do:

Step 1. Drive 7 nails into the plank of wood such that each successive nail is a little further in the wood than the one before it.

Step 2. Drive one nail into the small block.

Step 3. Hit the nails on the plank with the single nail to play your 'nail piano'.

Step 4. You can even tune it by driving the nails further in or pulling them out!

💡 **What just happened?** Wood is a good conductor of sound. The wood transfers the vibrations caused by hitting one nail with the other.

192. Wailing Ruler

Duration of Experiment: 🕐 5 mins.   Difficulty Level: ▬▬ ═ ▆

What you need:

String   Ruler   Nail

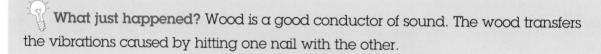

What to do:

Step 1. Use the nail to make a hole in at one end of the ruler or use a ruler that already has a hole in it. Tie the string to it.

Step 2. Hold the string and whirl the ruler around.

Step 3. You can hear a low pitched wailing sound.

💡 **What just happened?** When you whirl the ruler fast enough, the speed of the ruler is more than the speed of sound. This creates a sonic boom, which creates the sound.

193. Popsicle Stick Harmonica

Duration of Experiment: **30** mins.   Difficulty Level: ▬ ▬ ▬

What you need:

Ice cream sticks   Rubber band   Tape   Craft paper (2 strips about 3 cm × 1 cm)

What to do:

Step 1. Put one stick on top of the other.

Step 2. Cut out two strips from the craft paper, about 3 cm x 1 cm each.

Step 3. Tape the strips about 1.5 cm from each end. Make sure that the tape does not touch the sticks at all.

Step 4. Slide the bottom stick out.

Step 5. Stretch a rubber band along the length of the top stick.

Step 6. Place the bottom stick back in its place. The rubber band should go around the top stick only, not the bottom stick as well.

Step 7. Hold the 'harmonica' up to your lips and blow through it.

SCIENCE AROUND US

How do we talk?

The basis of all sounds is vibrations. Speech actually starts in the stomach with the diaphragm, which pushes air from the lungs into the voice box. This causes the strings in the voice box to vibrate, creating a sound. The tongue, lips, teeth and roof of the mouth help in shaping the sounds.

💡 **What just happened?** The air blowing through the rubber band makes it vibrate against the sticks, making the sound.

194. Dancing Wire

Duration of Experiment: ⏱ 10 mins.   Difficulty Level: ▬▬ ▬ ▬

What you need:

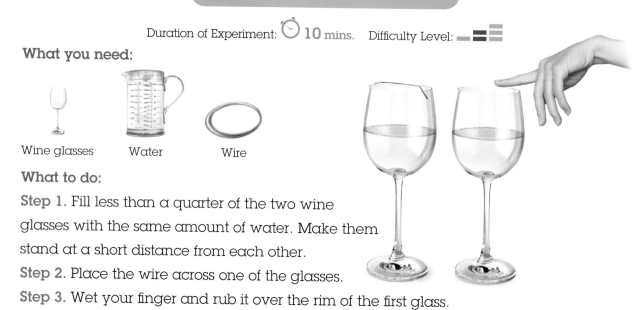

Wine glasses   Water   Wire

What to do:

Step 1. Fill less than a quarter of the two wine glasses with the same amount of water. Make them stand at a short distance from each other.

Step 2. Place the wire across one of the glasses.

Step 3. Wet your finger and rub it over the rim of the first glass.

Step 4. The wire on the second glass begins to jump around!

💡 **What just happened?** This phenomenon, in which an object begins to vibrate because another object in its vicinity is vibrating at the right frequency, is called 'resonance'.

195. Musical Buttons

Duration of Experiment: ⏱ 10 mins.   Difficulty Level: ▬▬ ▬ ▬

What you need:

Button   String

What to do:

Step 1. Thread the string through one button hole and bring it back up through the other. Tie the ends to form a loop.

Step 2. Bring the button to the centre of the string and stretch it out between both your pointer fingers.

Step 3 Wind up the string. Pull the string tight and loosen it.

💡 **What just happened?** The spinning button and the string are vibrating the air around them, making the singing sound.

196. Umbrella Speakers

Duration of Experiment: ⏱ **30** mins.   Difficulty Level: ▬ ▬ ▬

What you need:

Two Stands   Tape   Watch   2 umbrellas   Nails

What to do:

Step 1. Place two open umbrellas outdoors, around 2.5 metres apart. Their handles should face each other.

Step 2. Use the stand and nails to fix the handles of the umbrellas to the ground with the umbrella placed on the ground such that the handles are parallel to the ground.

Step 3. Place the watch at different spots in the umbrella and notice at which spot the ticking is the loudest. Tape the ticking watch to that spot.

Step 4. Place your ear at the corresponding spot on the other umbrella.

Step 5. You can hear the clock ticking!

💡 **What just happened?** The sound waves from the watch are amplified because of the shape of the umbrella. These waves bounce off the first umbrella and hit the other umbrella. The sound then bounces off the corresponding spot on the other umbrella, which is why you can hear it.

197. Doctor Doctor

Duration of Experiment: 15 mins. Difficulty Level: ▬ ▬▬ ▦

What you need:

2 Funnels   Garden hose   Scissors   Clay

What to do:

Step 1. Cut about 16 inches of the garden hose.

Step 2. Place the funnels on both ends of the hose.

Step 3. Use modelling clay to secure the funnel over the hose.

Step 4. Place one end of the funnel on your heart and the other on your ear.

What just happened? You just heard your heartbeat! Sound waves travel through the hose and are amplified by the funnel because of its shape.

198. Blowing Whistles

Duration of Experiment: 10 mins. Difficulty Level: ▬ ▬▬ ▦

What you need:

Straws (One should be thicker than the other)   Scissors

What to do:

Step 1. Flatten one end of the thinner straw.

Cut a pointed 'V'.

Step 2. Insert the other end into the thicker straw.

Step 3. Blow into the 'V'.

Step 4. Change the length of the straw. The sound changes!

What just happened? The sound is created by the two flaps vibrating. These vibrations travel only a short distance when the straw is short, but a longer distance when you elongate the straw. This causes the differences in the pitch of sound.

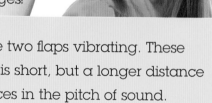

199. Make a Kazoo

Duration of Experiment: 20 mins.   Difficulty Level:

What you need:

Pencil   Rubber band   Tissue paper   Cardboard tube

What to do:

Step 1. Place tissue over one end of the cardboard tube. Secure it with a rubber band.

Step 2. Use the pencil to make a hole in the cardboard tube near this end.

Step 3. Hum into the other end of the roll to create a comical sound.

 What just happened? Humming or speaking into the cardboard tube makes the tissue at the bottom vibrate. All these vibrations can only escape through the small hole. This is why the sound is loud.

200. Cardboard Xylophone

Duration of Experiment: 20 mins.   Difficulty Level:

What you need:

String   8 cardboard tubes   Shoebox   Hammer   Scissors

What to do:

Step 1. Cut the cardboard tubes such that each one is slightly shorter than the previous one.

Step 2. Tie the tubes one below the other with the longest one on top and shortest one at the bottom.

Step 3. Tie this to the ends of a shoe box.

Step 4. Use the small hammer to hit the tubes to create different sounds.

What just happened? The longer tubes make a deeper sound than the shorter ones because they have more space inside for the sound to vibrate.

201. Whistling Funnel

Duration of Experiment: ⏱ 15 mins.   Difficulty Level: ▬▬ ▬▬ ▬▬

What you need:

Whistle   String   Funnel

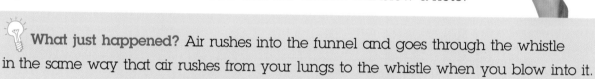

What to do:

Step 1. Insert the end of a whistle into the funnel.

Step 2. Tie one end of the string to the funnel and the other to the whistle.

Step 3. Whirl this around in a circle and the whistle will blow a note.

💡 **What just happened?** Air rushes into the funnel and goes through the whistle in the same way that air rushes from your lungs to the whistle when you blow into it.

202. Hydrophone

Duration of Experiment: ⏱ 15 mins.   Difficulty Level: ▬▬ ▬▬ ▬▬

What you need:

Scissors   Water   Tub   Stones   Large plastic bottle

What to do:

Step 1. Cut the bottom of the bottle off.

Step 2. Fill the tub with water.

Step 3. Place the bottle in the water.

Step 4. Put your ear to the top of the bottle.

Step 5. Bang two stones together under the water near the bottle.

Step 6. The sound will be magnified.

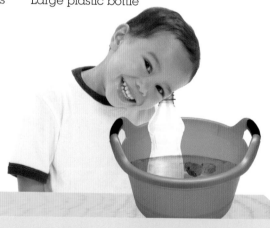

💡 **What just happened?** Sound travels faster through denser material. As water is denser than air, it travels faster and sounds louder underwater.

203. Make a Megaphone

Duration of Experiment: ⏱ 15 mins.   Difficulty Level: ▬ ▬ ▬

What you need:

Tape   Paper

What to do:

Step 1. Roll the paper into a cone.

Step 2. Stick the edge with the help of tape to secure it.

Step 3. Speak into the cone.

Step 4. Listen as your voice is louder!

Step 5. Put the cone to your ear and you will be able to hear everything louder!

💡 **What just happened?** The shape of the cone is such that it enhances sound. Sound bounces off the walls of the funnel and is concentrated through the small opening, which amplifies it.

204. Shake it!

Duration of Experiment: ⏱ 30 mins.   Difficulty Level: ▬ ▬ ▬

What you need:

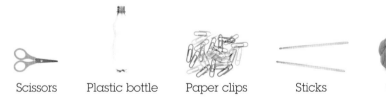

Scissors   Plastic bottle   Paper clips   Sticks   Clay

What to do:

Step 1. Put the paper clips in the bottle and screw the cap on.

Make a hole in the cap using the scissors, wide enough for the stick to fit.

Step 2. Fix the stick there with the help of some clay.

Step 3. Hold your 'rattle' by the stick and shake it to observe the different kinds of sounds.

💡 **What just happened?** The paper clips hit the edge of the bottle, creating the sound. If you change the material put in the bottle, the sound created changes.

125

UNDER PRESSURE
Experiments on the principle of air pressure

'Air pressure', as the name rightly suggests, is the pressure constantly exerted by the air that surrounds us. The unit of pressure is 'atmosphere' and is denoted by 'kgf'. There is a pressure of 1 kgf on every square centimetre. This means that a weight of 200 kgf presses down on your hand at every moment!

In fact, the phrase 'as light as air' is technically very misleading because a cubic metre of air weighs about 1.3 kg. The weight of all the air on Earth is 5,000,000,000,000,000,000,000 kg!

205. Stab the Potato

Duration of Experiment: ⏱ 5 mins.   Difficulty Level: ▬ ▬ ▬

What you need:

Straw   Potato

What to do:

Step 1. Try to stab the potato using the straw. It won't be easy.

Step 2. Now, place your thumb over the top of the straw and try to stab the potato.

Step 3. It's much easier to stab the potato this time!

💡 **What just happened?** Covering the top of the straw with your thumb traps the air inside, forcing it to compress as you stab the straw through the potato skin. This makes the straw strong enough to pierce the potato.

206. Build a Hovercraft

Duration of Experiment: ⏱ **40** mins.   Difficulty Level: ▬▬ ▬▬ ▬▬

What you need:

CD   Balloon   Glue   Drill   Bottle cap

What to do:

Step 1. Make a hole in the bottle cap using the drill.

Step 2. Glue the cap to the centre of the CD.

Step 3. Seal it so that air cannot escape.

Step 4. Fit the neck of the blown balloon over the cap.

Step 5. Put your hovercraft on a smooth surface and see it effortlessly glides across.

💡 **What just happened?** The air flow created by the balloon causes a cushion of moving air between the disc and the surface. This lifts the CD and reduces the friction.

207. Straw-struck

Duration of Experiment: ⏱ **5** mins.   Difficulty Level: ▬▬ ▬▬ ▬▬

What you need:

Straws   Glass   Soft drink

What to do:

Step 1. Fill the glass with the soft drink.

Step 2. Put one end of both the straws in your mouth.

Step 3. Put the other end of one straw in the drink and leave the second straw in the air and try to drink.
It's impossible because all you get are mouthfuls of air!

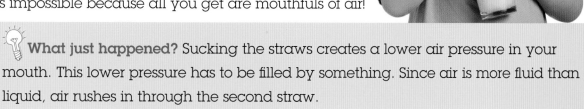

💡 **What just happened?** Sucking the straws creates a lower air pressure in your mouth. This lower pressure has to be filled by something. Since air is more fluid than liquid, air rushes in through the second straw.

208. Can Spin

Duration of Experiment: 30 mins.   Difficulty Level:

What you need:

Nail   String   Water   Candle   Matchsticks   Can   Bucket

What to do:

Step 1. Make a hole in the middle of one side of the unopened can. Turn the nail to the right until it lies flat against the can.

Step 2. Make a second hole on the opposite side of the can. Again, turn the nail to the right until it lies flat against the can to create a hole facing the right.

Step 3. Drain all of the soft drink from the can.

Step 4. Fill the bucket with water.

Step 5. Push the can into the bucket and fill it till up to a quarter.

Step 6. Tie the string to the top of the can so that it hangs.

Step 7. Light the candle.

Step 8. Hold the can over the candle till the water starts boiling and the can spins.

SCIENCE AROUND US

How do steam engines work?

A steam engine is a type of machine that gets energy from steam. Energy from a steam engine comes from the heat of the boiler, which works much like a huge pot filled with water. This is just a more elaborate form of your spinning can!

What just happened? When water boils, it turns into steam. The steam inside the can builds up pressure and starts to push out through the holes in the side of the can. This marks the can spin.

209. Thirsty Candle

Duration of Experiment: ⏱ **20** mins.   Difficulty Level: ▬▬ ▬

What you need:

Bowl   Food co-louring   Water   Candle   Matchsticks   Glass

What to do:

Step 1. Fill very little water in the bowl. Add two drops of food colouring to it.

Step 2. Place the candle in the middle of the bowl and light it.

Step 3. Turn the glass over and place it over the candle.

Step 4. Watch as the coloured water gets sucked into the glass.

> 💡 **What just happened?** When the candle burns inside the glass, the air inside the glass expands, creating a higher air pressure. The high pressure air inside tries to move towards the lower pressure air outside, creating space for the water to get 'sucked' in.

210. Collapsing Cans

Duration of Experiment: ⏱ **20** mins.   Difficulty Level: ▬ ▬ ▬

What you need:

Can   Tongs   Saucepan   Water

What to do:

Step 1. Fill the saucepan with cold water.

Step 2. Put a tablespoon of water into the empty can.

Step 3. Heat the can on the kitchen stove to boil the water.

Step 4. Invert the can in the saucepan with the tongs. It will collapse almost instantaneously.

> 💡 **What just happened?** The vapour from the boiling water pushed air out of the can. When it was suddenly cooled by inverting it in the water, the vapour condensed, forming a vacuum. The low pressure in the can allowed the pressure outside to crush it.

211. Balloon Powered Car

Duration of Experiment: ⏱ **45** mins.   Difficulty Level: ▬ ▬ ▬

What you need:

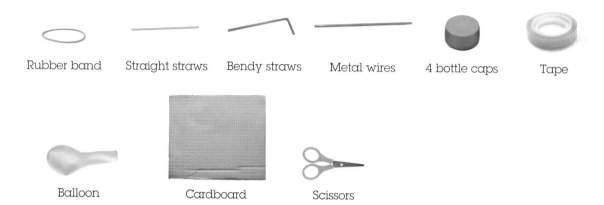

Rubber band   Straight straws   Bendy straws   Metal wires   4 bottle caps   Tape

Balloon   Cardboard   Scissors

What to do:

Step 1. Tape the straight straws horizontally across the cardboard on opposite ends.

Step 2. Push the wire through these straws.

Step 3. Make a hole in the bottle caps and push them into the wire, to create wheels.

Step 4. Cut a bendy straw in half.

Step 5. Tie the balloon to one end of this straw with the rubber band.

Step 6. Tape the bendy straw to the cardboard.

Step 7. Blow the balloon through the straw and leave it on a smooth surface to see the car move forward.

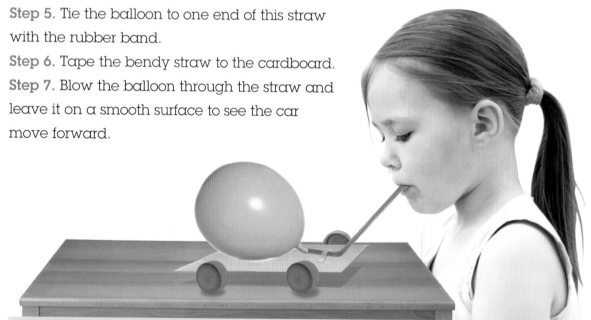

💡 **What just happened?** After you put the car on a surface and let go of the straw, the air moves out of the straw in one direction and the car moves in the opposite direction.

212. Stubborn Balls

Duration of Experiment: ⏱ 5 mins.   Difficulty Level: ▬ ▬ ▬

What you need:

Paper

Plastic bottle

What to do:

Step 1. Lay the bottle horizontally.

Step 2. Make a small paper ball, about half the size
of the mouth of the bottle.

Step 3. Place the ball at the mouth of the bottle and try to blow it in.

Step 4. No matter how hard you blow, the ball comes shooting back out at you!

💡 **What just happened?** Moving air has a lower pressure than still air. When you
were blowing on the ball, the air is deflected around the sides of the bottle.
This makes the paper ball come shooting out every time you blow on it.

213. Attractive Apples

Duration of Experiment: ⏱ 10 mins.   Difficulty Level: ▬ ▬ ▬

What you need:

Apples

String

What to do:

Step 1. Tie the string to the stems of two apples.

Step 2. Hang the two apples by a clothesline or curtain
rod, two inches away from each other.

Step 3. Blow between the apples. They get attracted
to each other!

💡 **What just happened?** When you blow in the middle of the two apples, the
air pressure between them becomes lower. This makes the still air push the two
apples together.

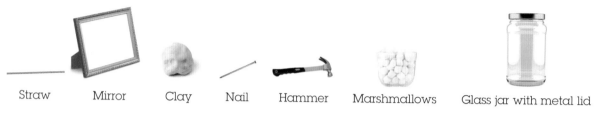

214. Marshy Mellows

Duration of Experiment: ⏱ **20** mins.   Difficulty Level: ▬ ▬ ▬

What you need:

Straw   Mirror   Clay   Nail   Hammer   Marshmallows   Glass jar with metal lid

What to do:

Step 1. Use the nail to make a hole in the middle of the metal lid.

Step 2. Put the straw through the hole in the lid and seal it with the clay.

Step 3. Drop the marshmallows in the jar and shut the lid.

Step 4. Hold the mirror such that you can see the marshmallows.

Step 5. Blow air into the jar and watch them shrink!

SCIENCE AROUND US

How are marshmallows made?

Marshmallows are mostly sugar and water wrapped around a bunch of air bubbles. This is why they are so soft and spongy. If you were to microwave a marshmallow, the air pockets would expand and the marshmallow would grow to four times its size!
Try it out!

💡 **What just happened?** Marshmallows have a lot of air pockets. They are not a solid object. By blowing air into the jar, you increased the pressure within the jar, crushing the air pockets and making the marshmallow reduce in size.

215. Spraying Fountain

Duration of Experiment: ⏱ **30 mins.**   Difficulty Level: ▬▬▬

What you need:

Drill   2 glass jars   Straws   Water   Food colouring   Baking pan   Clay

What to do:

Step 1. Drill two holes in the lid of one jar.

Step 2. Insert both straws through the holes—one should remain two inches above the lid, and the other two inches below.

Step 3. Seal them with the clay.

Step 4. Fill half the jar with water. Add yellow food colouring to it.

Step 5. Fill half of another jar with water. Add blue food colouring to it.

Step 6. Place the jar with blue water in the baking pan.

Step 7. Turn the jar with the straws upside down. Place the longer straw in the jar.

Step 8. Let the yellow water empty into the pan through the long straw. You will soon notice a pretty blue fountain!

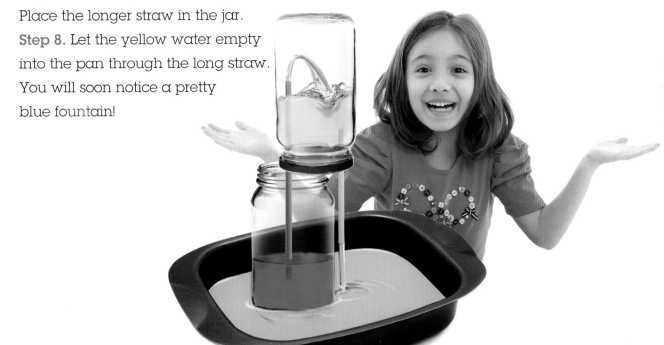

💡 **What just happened?** As the yellow water from the sealed jar empties out through the straw, the air pressure inside the jar reduces. Air pressure then forces the blue water to spray out of the shorter straw.

216. Windy Balloons

Duration of Experiment: 10 mins.   Difficulty Level: ▬ ▬▬ ▬

What you need:

Balloon   Hair dryer

What to do:

Step 1. Blow up the balloon.

Step 2. Turn on the hair dryer.

Step 3. Point the hair dryer upward and put the balloon on top of it.

Step 4. See if you can guide the movement of the balloon with the hair dryer.

What just happened? The moving air exerts a lower pressure than the still air around the balloon. Hence, the balloon gets pulled towards the hairdryer instead of getting blown away.

217. Glass of Air

Duration of Experiment: 10 mins.   Difficulty Level: ▬ ▬▬ ▬

What you need:

Glasses   Tray   Water

What to do:

Step 1. Pour some water into the tray.

Step 2. Lay the glass in the tray so that it fills with water completely.

Step 3. Raise the glass upside down. Make sure the mouth remains underwater.

Step 4. The water remains in the glass!

What just happened? The air around exerts pressure on the water, which forces the water into the glass.

218. Sticky Plate

Duration of Experiment: ⏱ 5 mins.   Difficulty Level: ▬▬ ▬▬ ▬▬

What you need:

Small plate   Jar   Paper towel   Paper   Water   Matchsticks

What to do:

Step 1. Wet the paper towel and fold it into a square or rectangle that is slightly wider than the mouth of the jar.

Step 2. Lay it flat in the centre of the plate.

Step 3. Tear a piece of paper, light it and drop it in the jar.

Step 4. Turn the jar over onto the wet paper towel and hold it in place till the paper stops burning. Lift the jar. The plate gets lifted too!

💡 **What just happened?** When you drop the burning paper in the jar, the air pressure inside increases. Once this air cools, the pressure decreases. This creates a vacuum.

219. Balloon Rocket

Duration of Experiment: ⏱ 20 mins.   Difficulty Level: ▬▬ ▬▬ ▬▬

What you need:

Balloon   String   Stool   Straw   Tape

What to do:

Step 1. Tie one end of the string to a chair or stool.

Step 2. Put the other end of the string through the straw.

Step 3. Pull the string tight.

Step 4. Blow up the balloon, pinch the end and tape the balloon to the straw.

Step 5. Let go and watch the rocket fly!

💡 **What just happened?** The air rushes out of the balloon, making it move forward. This sort of force is called 'thrust'.

220. Make Your Own Barometer

Duration of Experiment: ⏱ 20 mins.   Difficulty Level: ▬ ■ ▬

What you need:

Bottle   Dish   Paper   Water

What to do:

Step 1. Fill $\frac{3}{4}^{th}$ of the bottle with water. Fill half the dish with water.

Step 2. Hold your thumb over the bottle's mouth. Invert it into the dish.

Step 3. Stick a strip of paper with markings on the bottle.

Step 4. When the air pressure is high, you will find that the level of water in the bottle is higher than when the pressure is low.

💡 **What just happened?** Higher air pressure forces more water into the bottle and lower pressure allows more water in the dish. This causes the fluctuations in the water level.

221. The Hungry Bottle

Duration of Experiment: ⏱ 10 mins.   Difficulty Level: ▬ ■ ▬

What you need:

Matchsticks   Oil   Paper   Banana   Glass bottle

What to do:

Step 1. Tear the paper into small pieces. Dip them in oil.

Step 2. Put these in the bottle.

Step 3. Drop a lit matchstick in the bottle.

Step 4. Quickly place the banana over the bottle with the flesh in the bottle, and the peels at the sides.

Step 5. Watch the bottle eat the banana hungrily!

💡 **What just happened?** The burning paper used up all the oxygen in the bottle. This caused a lower pressure in the bottle. The air pressure outside was sufficient to push the banana into the bottle.

222. Straw Fountain

Duration of Experiment: ○ 5 mins.   Difficulty Level: ▬▬ ▬ ▬

What you need:

———————

Straw   Cork   Bottle   Water   Nail

What to do:

Step 1. Make a hole in the cork large enough for the straw to fit in.

Step 2. Fill half the bottle with water and cork it. Put the straw in.

Step 3. Blow into the straw and immediately move your head away.

Step 4. Water comes spurting out.

💡 **What just happened?** By blowing, you compressed the air inside the bottle, increasing the pressure. When you stopped, the compressed air expanded again, pushing the water back up the straw.

223. Stuck Glasses

Duration of Experiment: ○ 10 mins.   Difficulty Level: ▬▬ ▬ ▬

What you need:

Rubber ring   Glasses   Paper   Matchsticks

What to do:

Step 1. Wet the ring and lay it on top of one of the glasses.

Step 2. Drop a bit of burning paper into the glass and immediately put the other glass upside down over this glass.

Step 3. When the paper stops burning, you will notice that they are both stuck to each other.

💡 **What just happened?** Burning the paper causes a lower air pressure inside the two glasses. The greater pressure of the air outside causes the glasses to remain tightly stuck to each other.

224. Potato Cannon

Duration of Experiment: 10 mins.   Difficulty Level:

What you need:

Potato slices   Cardboard tube   Pencil

What to do:

Step 1. Push one end of the tube through a slice of potato. The slice should stick to the tube, completely covering it.

Step 2. Do the same with the other end.

Step 3. Use the pencil to swiftly push the potato from one side of the tube.

Step 4. The potato at the other end will fly out.

What just happened? You just made an elementary air gun! You compress the air in the tube by pushing the potato in from one end.

225. Flame Killer

Duration of Experiment: 20 mins.   Difficulty Level:

What you need:

Candle   Bowl   Cooking vinegar   Baking powder   Matchsticks   Jar with a hole in the lid

What to do:

Step 1. Place the lit candle in the middle of the bowl.

Step 2. Fill $\frac{1}{4}^{th}$ of the jar with baking powder. Pour vinegar till the jar is halfway full. Immediately, shake the jar carefully. The mixture will start fizzing and popping. Now, point the hole of the jar towards the candle flame. The flame goes off.

What just happened? A flame needs oxygen to continue burning. The baking powder and vinegar reacted to form a gas called carbon dioxide. Carbon dioxide does not allow the flame to continue burning.

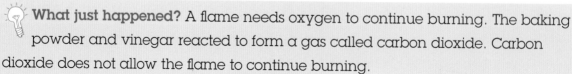

226. Deflating Balloons

Duration of Experiment: ⏱ 10 mins.   Difficulty Level: ▬ ▬ ▬

What you need:

2 balloons

Rubber hose

What to do:

Step 1. Blow up one of the balloons to a normal size. Ask someone to hold it.

Step 2. Blow the other balloon to half that size.

Step 3. Put both the balloons on opposite ends of the tube. Don't leave the neck of the balloons.

Step 4. Once they are comfortably fitted, leave both at the same time and see what happens. Contrary to what you expect, the small balloon deflates completely.

💡 **What just happened?** Though you'd expect the big balloon to push air into the smaller one, the opposite happens. Air always moves from high pressure to low pressure. The pressure in the smaller balloon is higher than the bigger one, and so the air moves from the small balloon to the big one.

227. Air Lift

Duration of Experiment: 10 mins. Difficulty Level: ▬ ▆▆ ▆▆

What you need:

Balloon

Book

Table

What to do:

Step 1. Put the balloon on a table, but let the open end of it hang off the edge.

Step 2. Put the book on the balloon so that it is covering half the balloon.

Step 3. Now blow the balloon. The balloon will be strong enough to lift the book.

What just happened? By blowing into the balloon you are increasing the air pressure in it. This is greater than the air pressure being exerted on the book. So, it is easy to lift the book.

228. Balloon in a Bottle

Duration of Experiment: 10 mins. Difficulty Level: ▬ ▆▆ ▆▆

What you need:

Balloon

Plastic bottle

Pin

What to do:

Step 1. Put the balloon in the bottle.
Cover the mouth of the bottle with the balloon.

Step 2. Try to blow the balloon. You will not be able to.

Step 3. Now poke a hole at the bottom of the bottle and try again. You can now blow the balloon.

What just happened? Without the hole, the air inside the bottle is exerting pressure on the balloon, making it impossible to blow. Once you made a hole, the balloon was able to push the air from the bottle out to make space.

229. Floating Ball

Duration of Experiment: 10 mins.   Difficulty Level:

What you need:

Bendy straw

Ping-pong ball

What to do:

Step 1. Bend the straw into an L shape.

Step 2. Put the longer end of the straw in your mouth.

Step 3. Hold the ping-pong ball over the short end of the straw and blow. See your ping-pong ball levitate!

What just happened? Moving air is at a lower pressure than still air. So, the ball is surrounded by a higher pressure. This ensures that the balloon remains over the straw.

230. Balloon Lift

Duration of Experiment: 15 mins.   Difficulty Level:

What you need:

Balloon

Paper

Jar

Matchsticks

What to do:

Step 1. Blow the balloon such that it is slightly larger than the mouth of the jar.

Step 2. Light the piece of paper and drop it in the jar.

Step 3. Place the balloon on top of the jar.

Step 4. When the fire goes out, pick up the balloon. The jar is lifted as well!

What just happened? The air gets used up by the flame. This lowers the air pressure inside the jar. The surrounding air outside, now at a higher pressure than the air inside the jar, pushes the balloon into the jar.

231. Balloon Surfer

Duration of Experiment: 🕐 **20** mins.   Difficulty Level: ▬ ▬ ▬

What you need:

Balloon   Bottle cap   Nail   Tub   Water

What to do:

Step 1. Make a hole in the bottle cap with the nail.

Step 2. Blow the balloon. Do not tie it.

Step 3. Stretch it over the cap, still holding it from the neck.

Step 4. Place it in a tub of water and watch it go!

💡 **What just happened?** When the balloon is left, the air rushes out through the small hole in the cap. This propels the entire device forward.

232. Rocket Pinwheel

Duration of Experiment: 🕐 **20** mins.   Difficulty Level: ▬ ▬ ▬

What you need:

Bendy straw   Balloon   Tape   Pencil (with an eraser   Pin
                                   on the end)

What to do:

Step 1. Tape the balloon to the long end of the bendy straw.

Step 2. Attach the straw from the middle to the bottom of the pencil with the pin.

Step 3. Blow the balloon through one end of the straw.

Step 4. Release it and watch your pinwheel spin!

💡 **What just happened?** When the air is pushed out from the balloon, it travels all through the straw and comes out from the other end of the straw. It pushes against the air that is already there. This powers the pinwheel.

233. Dry Newspaper

Duration of Experiment: 10 mins.   Difficulty Level: ▬ ▬▬ ▬▬

What you need:

Newspaper   Glass   Bowl

What to do:

Step 1. Stuff a sheet of newspaper into the glass. Make sure it is packed tight but do not let it come all the way up to the rim of the glass.

Step 2. Turn the glass over and submerge it straight into the bowl. Do not tilt the glass.

Step 3. Hold it there for 10 seconds and take it out. Your newspaper sheet is as dry as the Sahara desert!

💡 **What just happened?** There is a layer of air between the newspaper and the water. This layer exerts pressure on the water and does not let it touch the newspaper.

234. Sprayer

Duration of Experiment: 15 mins.   Difficulty Level: ▬ ▬▬ ▬▬

What you need:

Straws   Glass   Water

What to do:

Step 1. Put a straw in half a glass of water.

Step 2. Hold the other straw at a 90° angle to this one. Blow hard.

Step 3. You will notice the water level rising in the straw.

Step 4. Blow long enough, and it will soon look like a hairspray.

💡 **What just happened?** When you blow on top of the straw, it creates a lower pressure, making the water rise in the straw.

THE AIRY GODMOTHER

Experiments involving the other properties of air

Air is everywhere all the time, though we cannot see, hear or feel it. In fact, most often we don't even notice its presence. But try holding your breath for more than a minute or two and you'll definitely notice its absence!

This section deals with the various properties of air. Among many other things, you will also learn five unconventional methods of inflating a balloon without touching it to your mouth.

235. Incredible Hoop Glider

Duration of Experiment: ⏱ 15 mins.　Difficulty Level: ▬ ▬ ▬

What you need:

Straw　　　Card paper　　　Tape　　　Scissors

What to do:

Step 1. Cut the card paper into three strips (2.5 cm × 13 cm).

Step 2. Make one large loop out of two strips.

Step 3. Make a smaller loop out of the third strip.

Step 4. Tape both the loops to the ends of the straw.

Step 5. Hold your glider by the straw, angle it upwards and launch it into the air!

💡 **What just happened?** The two loops keep the straw balanced. The large loop creates a 'drag' which keeps it airborne, and the smaller one keeps it from turning off course.

236. Bubble Within a Bubble

Duration of Experiment: 15 mins.   Difficulty Level:

What you need:

Plastic cup   Wire loop   Straw   Bubble mix   Water

What to do:

Step 1. In case bubble mix isn't available, you can make your own mix by mixing water, washing soap and glycerine.

Step 2. Turn the cup upside down and place it on a flat surface like a table.

Step 3. Wet the surface of the cup with water.

Step 4. Use the wire loop to blow a bubble on the base of the cup, which is now on top.

Step 5. Wet the straw with the bubble liquid by dipping the straw in the liquid.

Step 6. Gently slide it into the bubble and blow a smaller bubble. You now have a bubble inside a bubble!

SCIENCE AROUND US

How do bubbles form?

Bubbles are pockets of soap and water that are filled with air. When soap and water are mixed together and air is blown into the mixture, the soap forms a thin skin or wall and traps the air, creating a bubble.

What just happened? Bubbles are air trapped within a liquid ball. Contact with a dry surface makes it burst. An object that is wet and soapy itself can easily enter the bubble without bursting it.

237. Air Twirly

Duration of Experiment: ⏱ 10 mins. Difficulty Level: ▬ ▬ ▬

What you need:

Pencil (with an eraser at the end)   Paper   Pin   Eraser   Scissors

What to do:

Step 1. Cut a square out of the paper. Fold it along the diagonals.

Step 2. Stick the tip of the pencil in the eraser and stick the pin into the bottom of the pencil.

Step 3. Place the centre of the paper on the pin.

Step 4. Rub your hands together and place them below the paper. The paper starts spinning!

💡 **What just happened?** The warmth from your hands heated the air around it, which began to rise, causing the twirly to spin.

238. Eggs-periment

Duration of Experiment: ⏱ 10 mins. Difficulty Level: ▬ ▬ ▬

What you need:

Boiled egg   Plastic bottle   Bowls   Water

What to do:

Step 1. Put the bottle in the bowl of hot water for about five minutes.

Step 2. Move the bottle to the bowl of ice water. Wet the egg and place it pointed side down in the bottle opening. The egg gets sucked into the bottle!

💡 **What just happened?** When the air in the bottle is heated, the air pressure in the bottle increases. As it cools, the pressure decreases. The air pressure from outside pushes the egg into the bottle.

239. Bendy Air Trick

Duration of Experiment: ⏱ 5 mins.   Difficulty Level: ▬ ▬ ▬

What you need:

Paper   Tape   Book   Bottle   Water   Scissors   Table

What to do:

Step 1. Cut the paper into a strip (2 cm × 10 cm). Fold one end.

Step 2. Tape the paper to the table such that the longer portion of the strip is standing perpendicular to the table.

Step 3. Place the book between yourself and the paper. Try to make the paper flutter by blowing on the book. You won't be able to do so.

Step 4. Fill half the bottle with water and place it where the book was. The paper will flutter.

SCIENCE AROUND US

Aerodynamics

This property of air to 'bend' around curved objects is the reason why ships, cars and aeroplanes are the shape that they are. The streamlined shape of planes and ships allow them to move faster.

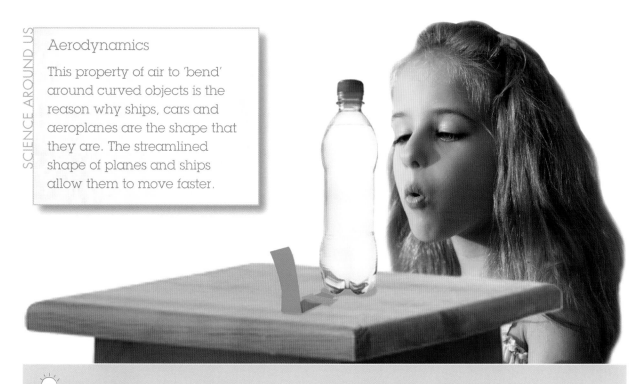

💡 **What just happened?** The book blocks the air that you are blowing. The air deflects back at right angles. But the air bends around the curved surface of the bottle, causing the paper to flutter.

240. Smoggy

Duration of Experiment: 10 mins.   Difficulty Level:

What you need:

Jar	Water	Aluminium foil	Ice cubes	Paper	Matchsticks

What to do:

Step 1. Make a 'lid' for the jar with the aluminium foil.

Step 2. Take it off and wet the insides of the jar with the water.

Step 3. Put a few scraps of burning paper in the jar.

Step 4. Immediately seal the jar with aluminium foil and put
the ice cubes on top. The air inside the jar will soon look smoggy.

What just happened? The burning paper caused some of the water in the jar to evaporate. This water vapour then rose and condensed back into drops of water when it came into contact with the foil.

241. Snake Spiral

Duration of Experiment: 10 mins.   Difficulty Level:

What you need:

Paper	Scissors	Pin	Pencil (with an eraser at the end)

What to do:

Step 1. Draw a spiral on the paper and cut it out.

Step 2. Loosely pin one end of the spiral to the rubber on top of the eraser.

Step 3. Hold the pencil over a stove.

Step 4. Watch the spiral begin to twirl!

What just happened? The hot air above the
stove rises, causing the spiral to rise along with it.

242. Air Scales

Duration of Experiment: 🕐 10 mins   Difficulty Level: ▬ ▬ ▬

What you need:

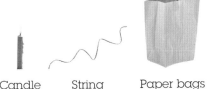
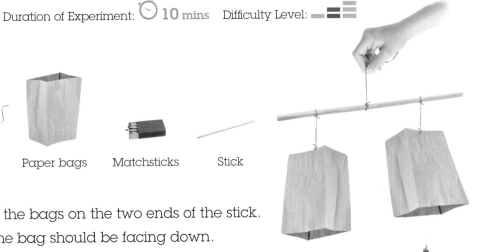

Candle   String   Paper bags   Matchsticks   Stick

What to do:

Step 1. Hang both the bags on the two ends of the stick. The open end of the bag should be facing down.

Step 2. Tie a string to the centre of the stick so that it balances horizontally.

Step 3. Hold the lighted candle below one of the bags.

Step 4. Watch as it slowly begins to rise.

💡 **What just happened?** The warm air rises, lifting the paper bag along with it.

243. Candle at the Door

Duration of Experiment: 🕐 10 mins.   Difficulty Level: ▬ ▬ ▬

What you need:

Candle   Matchsticks

What to do:

Step 1. Go into a warm room and leave the door partially open.

Step 2. Light the candle and hold it at the top of the door.

Step 3. You will be able to see the flame 'bend' towards the outside.

Step 4. Hold the candle at the bottom of the door.

Step 5. The flame bends 'inwards' this time.

💡 **What just happened?** The flame bends 'outward' at the top of the door because warm air rises and escapes out of the room.

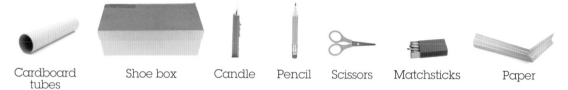
244. Obedient Smoke

Duration of Experiment: ⏱ 15 mins.   Difficulty Level: ▬ ▬ ▬

What you need:

Cardboard tubes   Shoe box   Candle   Pencil   Scissors   Matchsticks   Paper

What to do:

Step 1. Place the tubes on the two edges of the shoe box lid.

Step 2. Trace the outline of the tubes.

Step 3. Cut out two circles in the lid of the shoe box to fit the tubes in.

Step 4. Fix the tubes in the lid. These will now function as 'chimneys'.

Step 5. Light the candle and place it exactly below one of the 'chimneys'.

Step 6. Twist a bit of paper, light it and blow it out.

Step 7. Hold the now smouldering paper over the chimney without the candle below it.

Step 8. The smoke obediently comes up from the other chimney (the one with the candle under it).

💡 **What just happened?** The candle uses all the oxygen in the box and therefore draws in more air from the other tube. The smoke from the paper is also drawn into the box in this manner. It then gets heated in the box and rises out of the chimney along with the warm air.

245. Smoke Rings

Duration of Experiment: ⏱ 15 mins.   Difficulty Level: ▬ ▬ ▬

What you need:

Cling wrap   Tape   Talcum powder   Shoe box   Scissors

What to do:

Step 1. Cut off one side of the shoe box and replace it with cling wrap.

Step 2. Cut a hole on the opposite side of the box.

Step 3. Put some talcum powder in the box.

Step 4. Tap on the plastic covered side and watch the rings form!

SCIENCE AROUND US

Vortices

The scientific name for your 'smoke rings' is vortices. Vortices occur when liquids or gases spin or flow in a circular manner. Vortices usually occur in water but they sometimes occur in air.

💡 **What just happened?** The powder takes the form of doughnut-like shapes on its way out. Because the powder moves slower than the air, it maintains its shape.

246. Self-inflating Balloon

Duration of Experiment: **20** mins.   Difficulty Level: ▬▬ ▬▬ ▬▬

What you need:

| Empty bottle | Balloon | Water | Pan |

What to do:

Step 1. Stretch the balloon over the mouth of the empty bottle.

Step 2. Put the bottle in the pan of hot water for a few minutes.

Step 3. You should be able to see the balloon inflating soon.

💡 **What just happened?** As the air inside the bottle starts getting heated, it begins to expand. This air is trapped by the balloon, which begins stretching.

247. Blowing Balloons

Duration of Experiment: **20** mins.   Difficulty Level: ▬▬ ▬▬ ▬▬

What you need:

| Straw | Balloon | Plastic bottle | Water | Lemon | Baking soda |

What to do:

Step 1. Pour the water into the plastic bottle.

Step 2. Add the teaspoon of baking soda and stir it around with the straw until it has dissolved.

Step 3. Squeeze a few drops of lemon in and quickly put the balloon over the mouth of the bottle.

Step 4. Watch as your balloon inflates.

💡 **What just happened?** Adding the lemon juice to the baking soda created a chemical reaction, which caused carbon dioxide to be released. The gas rose up and escaped the soft drink bottle. However, it got trapped in the balloon.

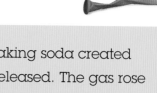

248. Balloon Expansion

Duration of Experiment: ⏱ 20 mins.   Difficulty Level: ▬▬ ▬▬ ▬▬

What you need:

| Yeast | Plastic bottle | 2 tsp. sugar | Water | Balloon |

What to do:

Step 1. Fill the bottle with an inch of warm water.

Step 2. Add yeast and gently swirl the bottle a few seconds.

Step 3. Add the sugar and swirl it around some more.

Step 4. Put the balloon over the neck of the bottle.
Set it aside in a warm place for 20 minutes.

Step 5. Watch the balloon expand!

💡 **What just happened?** As the yeast and sugar react, it releases a gas called carbon dioxide. The gas fills the bottle and then fills the balloon as more gas is created.

249. Balloon Blowing

Duration of Experiment: ⏱ 15 mins.   Difficulty Level: ▬▬ ▬▬ ▬▬

What you need:

| Antacid | Plastic bottle | Cooking vinegar | Balloon |

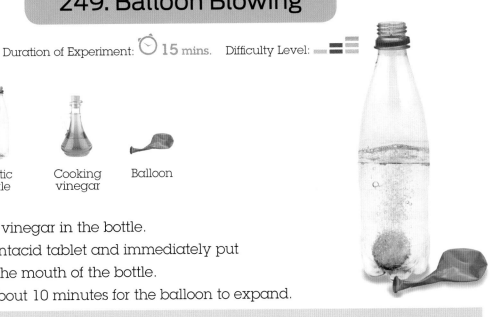

What to do:

Step 1. Put a little vinegar in the bottle.

Step 2. Drop an antacid tablet and immediately put
the balloon over the mouth of the bottle.

Step 3. Wait for about 10 minutes for the balloon to expand.

💡 **What just happened?** The vinegar and antacid react to form carbon dioxide. This carbon dioxide fills the space in the balloon, making it expand.

250. Inflating Balloons

Duration of Experiment: 10 mins.   Difficulty Level:

What you need:

Balloon   Soda bottle

What to do:

Step 1. Pour half the soda out.

Step 2. Put the balloon over the mouth of the soda bottle.

Step 3. Shake the bottle a little bit.

Step 4. Watch the balloon inflate!

What just happened? The small bubbles that you see in soda are carbon dioxide bubbles. When you shake the bottle, the gas is released and it fills the balloon.

251. Make a Hot Air Balloon

Duration of Experiment: 10 mins.   Difficulty Level:

What you need:

Duct tape   Large plastic bag   Hair dryer

What to do:

Step 1. Through the holes in the neck of the plastic bag seal it with duct tape to make the opening of the bag narrow.

Step 2. Blow hot air into the plastic bag using the hair dryer directed through the now small opening.

Step 3. After a few seconds, when the plastic bag is full of hot air, turn the hair dryer off and let go of the bag.

Step 4. The bag begins to rise towards the ceiling and hovers for some time.

What just happened? Hot air expands and rises, carrying your 'hot air balloon' along with it.

252. Air Surfing

Duration of Experiment: ⏱ 10 mins. Difficulty Level:

What you need:

Balloons   Table

What to do:

Step 1. Blow five balloons.

Step 2. Turn a small table over on them.

Step 3. You will find that you can stand comfortably on the table, even with another person!

💡 **What just happened?** When you stand on the table your weight is distributed among all the balloons, which is why they don't burst.

253. Magic Finger

Duration of Experiment: ⏱ 10 mins. Difficulty Level:

What you need:

Tin can   Drill   Water   Bowl

What to do:

Step 1. Use the drill to bore holes in the bottom of the can. Make one hole on the lid.

Step 2. Hold the can over the bowl and try to pour water in it. It drains out from the bottom.

Step 3. To stop the water from draining, you need to use your 'magic finger'.

Step 4. Pour water in the can, close the lid and quickly shut the hole with your finger.

💡 **What just happened?** By closing the lid, you stopped air from entering the can and the air outside the can presses upwards on the underside of the can to prevent the water from running out.

GO GREEN
Experiments with plants

Though they can't walk and talk like us, plants are living things.
They grow over a period of time.
There are some conditions that help them grow and some that don't.

Plants also have other interesting properties that are fun to study.
For example, did you know that you could grow a plant parallel to the ground?
Or that you can take the 'green' out of a leaf? Learn how to in this section!

254. Coloured Leaves

Duration of Experiment: 2 hours   Difficulty Level: ▬ ▬ ▬

What you need:

Spinach leaves

Glass jar

Acetone

Blotting paper

What to do:

Step 1. Mash the spinach leaves into a pulp. Place the pulp at the bottom of the glass jar.

Step 2. Cover all the spinach with acetone.

Step 3. Suspend a strip of the blotting paper into the jar.

Step 4. In a few hours, you will be able to see various colours separating themselves on the blotting paper.

💡 **What just happened?** The acetone extracted the pigments from the leaves. This was absorbed by the blotting paper by a process called capillary action. The acetone evaporated and left the pigments behind.

255. Why Leaves are Green

Duration of Experiment: ⏱ **7 days**   Difficulty Level: ▬ ▬ ▬

What you need:

Scissors   Clips   Plant   Black chart paper

What to do:

Step 1. Cover a few leaves with black chart paper.

Step 2. Put the plant where it can get plenty of sunlight.

Step 3. After a week, take the black paper off. The leaves you had covered are not as green as the others.

💡 **What just happened?** Leaves get their green colour from a substance that they produce, called 'chlorophyll'. Chlorophyll can be made only in the presence of sunlight. The leaf wrapped in chart paper did not get any sunlight.

256. Grow a Plant

Duration of Experiment: ⏱ **3 days**   Difficulty Level: ▬ ▬ ▬

What you need:

Sprouts   Cotton wool   Container   Water

What to do:

Step 1. Line the container with damp cotton.

Step 2. Place the sprouts on the damp cotton and leave it on a window sill.

Step 3. Every time the cotton dries up, dampen it again.

Step 4. The sprouts will grow in a few days.

💡 **What just happened?** You can see the sprout giving off small roots into the cotton, and a shoot begins to grow. Plants need water and sunlight to grow.

257. Leafy Oxygen

Duration of Experiment: 2 hours   Difficulty Level:

What you need:

Glass jar   Seaweed   Water

What to do:

Step 1. Fill the jar with water.

Step 2. Put the seaweed in the jar.

Step 3. Place the jar in a room with bright sunshine.

Step 4. Watch the jar closely. You will notice air bubbles rising.

What just happened? The air bubbles in the jar are oxygen. During the day, plants take in carbon dioxide and let out oxygen during photosynthesis.

258. Beanstalk

Duration of Experiment: 3 days   Difficulty Level:

What you need:

Beans   Glass jar   Cotton   Water

What to do:

Step 1. Fill half the jar with cotton.

Step 2. Put the beans on the cotton against the sides such that you can see them through the jar.

Step 3. Fill the rest of the jar with cotton.

Step 4. Pour water into the jar.

Step 5. Observe the various stages of germination over the next few days.

What just happened? Germination is the process by which plants emerge from seeds and begin to grow. The root always grows downward and the shoot upward.

259. Graft a Plant

Duration of Experiment: ⏱ **7 days**   Difficulty Level: ▬▬ ▬▬ ▬▬

What you need:

Craft knife   Modelling clay   Tomato plant   Potato plant   String

What to do:

Step 1. Pull the main stems of the potato and tomato plants together and tie them loosely with a string.

Step 2. Shave the bark till you can see the interior tubes.

Step 3. Tightly wrap string around the two shaved ends. Seal it with clay.

Step 4. After a week, cut off the old potato and old tomato plants above the wrapped part, creating a new 'pomato' plant.

💡 **What just happened?** This process is called plant 'grafting'. The new plant imbibes properties of both the old plants.

260. Smoky Prints

Duration of Experiment: ⏱ **30 mins.**   Difficulty Level: ▬▬ ▬▬ ▬▬

What you need:

Petroleum jelly   Glass bottle   Gloves   Newspaper   Candle   Leaf

Be careful while heating the bottle. Fire can be dangerous.

What to do:

Step 1. Spread petroleum jelly on the bottle and heat it over a flame using a glove. Heat it till it is covered with soot.

Step 2. Roll the sooty bottle over the veins of the leaf.

Step 3. Place the leaf between two sheets of paper.

Step 4. Roll a clean bottle over the sheets. Turn the paper over.

💡 **What just happened?** Petroleum jelly is a product that is made up of carbon. On heating, this carbon forms soot.

261. Carrot Top

Duration of Experiment: ⏱ **14** days   Difficulty Level: ▬ ▬ ☰

What you need:

Carrots   Dish   Knife   Soil

What to do:

Step 1. Cut half an inch off the tops (leafy part) of the carrots.

Step 2. Put the soil in the dish. Place the cut pieces of carrot in the bowl with the cut side facing down.

Step 3. In a few days, leaves start growing on the carrot tops.

💡 **What just happened?** The carrot is actually the root of the plant. It can sustain some foliage even though it does not regenerate itself completely.

262. Plant Sweat

Duration of Experiment: ⏱ **24** hours   Difficulty Level: ▬ ☰

What you need:

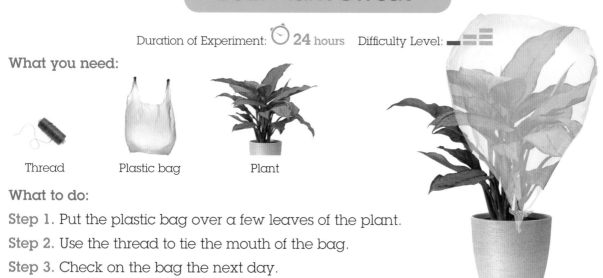

Thread   Plastic bag   Plant

What to do:

Step 1. Put the plastic bag over a few leaves of the plant.

Step 2. Use the thread to tie the mouth of the bag.

Step 3. Check on the bag the next day.

Step 4. You will notice that there are water droplets in the bag.

💡 **What just happened?** Plants lose water through their leaves in the form of water vapour. This vapour condenses in the plastic bag. This process is called 'transpiration'.

263. Potato Murderer

Duration of Experiment: **20** mins.   Difficulty Level:

What you need:

2 potatoes   Knife   1 tsp. sugar   Water   Dish

What to do:

Step 1. Boil one potato. This will 'kill' it.

Step 2. Slice off the top and bottom of both potatoes and scoop a hollow in each.

Step 3. Peel the lower half of each potato.

Step 4. Place the sugar in the hollow of each potato.

Step 5. Fill a dish with water and put both potatoes in it.

Step 6. Check the dish after 24 hours.

Step 7. The sugar in the boiled potato will remain the same but the sugar in the raw potato will be full of water.

SCIENCE AROUND US

Osmosis

In osmosis, liquids travel through a semi-permeable surface (like the potato skin). But potatoes aren't the only living things that can absorb water through their skin. Put your hand in water for 20 minutes and see what happens to your fingers!

What just happened? Water travels through the cell walls of living things. This process is called 'osmosis'. The cells in the boiled potato are dead, and so osmosis cannot take place.

264. Ink Prints

Duration of Experiment: 20 mins.   Difficulty Level: ▬ ▬ ▬

What you need:

Paint   White paper   Leaves   Paint tray   Rubber roller   Newspaper

What to do:

Step 1. Use the roller to spread some paint on a paint tray.

Step 2. Place the leaf, vein side up, on a newspaper.

Step 3. Roll over the leaf with the roller.

Step 4. Place the leaf ink side down on white paper and press it evenly. Remove the leaf to see the print.

💡 **What just happened?** The leaf is where most of the activity in the plant takes place. One can study its structure with the help of such prints.

265. Carbon Paper Leaf Prints

Duration of Experiment: 20 mins.   Difficulty Level: ▬ ▬ ▬

What you need:

Leaf   Petroleum jelly   Carbon paper   White sheets   Pen   Newspaper

What to do:

Step 1. Cover the veins of the leaf with petroleum jelly.

Step 2. Place it on a newspaper and cover with carbon paper.

Step 3. Cover the carbon paper with another sheet of paper. Rub it with the smooth side of a pen.

Step 4. Place the leaf between two sheets of white paper and rub it with the pen again.

💡 **What just happened?** The carbon from the carbon paper rubs off on the leaf and creates the print.

266. Carrot Hanging

Duration of Experiment: ○ 10 days   Difficulty Level: ▬ ▬ ▬

What you need:

String   Water   Knife   Long nail   Carrots

What to do:

Step 1. Choose a carrot that has a few leaves on its head.

Step 2. Cut about two inches from the top.

Step 3. Take help from an adult to hollow out the carrot top.

Step 4. Push the nail in horizontally and tie the string to both the ends of the nail.

Step 5. Fill the hollow with water.

Step 6. Hang your carrot hanging with the leaves pointing downwards.

Step 7. Keep refilling the hollow every time it gets dry.

Step 8. Soon the leaves will start growing upwards, against gravity.

SCIENCE AROUND US

Why do roots always grow downward?

No one knows exactly how, but plants are able to sense gravitational force.
The root always grows in the direction of the gravitational pull, while the shoot always grows against it. This is called 'gravitropism'.

💡 **What just happened?** The shoot of the plant will always grow against gravity. Since the carrot is actually the root of the plant, it absorbs water and transports it to the leaves. When the leaves get enough nutrition to grow, they grow against the force of gravity.

267. The Plant's Backbone

Duration of Experiment: ⏱ **14 days**   Difficulty Level: ▬▬ ■ ■

What you need:

2 tsp. baking soda   Books   Bowl   ½ cup bleach   Black cardboard   Leaves   Water

What to do:

Step 1. Mix two cups of warm water and baking soda in a shallow bowl.

Step 2. Submerge the leaves in this mixture.

Step 3. Leave the bowl in a sunny area for 12 days.

Step 4. Place the leaves between two pages of a book and leave it for two days.

Step 5. Mix the bleach with two cups of warm water and pour the mixture into a shallow bowl till the leaves whiten.

Step 6. Dry them and mount them on a black cardboard.

Step 7. You will be able to see the veins clearly.

💡 **What just happened?** Leaves make food for the plant. The food is made in the veins of the leaf. The stem absorbs and transports the baking soda solution to the veins. When we put the leaves in bleach, all the green pigment (chlorophyll) turned white, but the baking soda in the veins didn't.

268. Potato Obstacle

Duration of Experiment: 4 weeks   Difficulty Level:

What you need:

Shoe box

Potato (with shoots growing out of it)

Scissors

Soil

Small toys

What to do:

Step 1. Cut a small hole in one side of the shoe box.

Step 2. Put a little soil in the box, opposite the hole.

Step 3. Put the potato on the soil.

Step 4. Scatter the small toys around the box.

Step 5. Put the lid on and leave it on a window sill.

Step 6. Open it after four weeks. The shoot makes its way around the toys to the light.

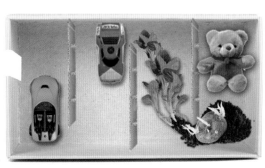

What just happened? Plant cells are sensitive to light and tell the plant which direction to grow in.

269. Anti-gravity Plants

Duration of Experiment: Variable   Difficulty Level:

What you need:

Seed

Soil

Pot

Water

What to do:

Step 1. Plant the seed in the pot of soil.

Step 2. Keep watering it till you see a shoot.

Step 3. Once the shoot is 4-5 inches tall, turn the plant over on its side.

Step 4. After a few weeks, the plant 'bends' and grows perpendicular to the ground!

What just happened? Plants grow against gravity regardless of what position they are in. Changing its orientation caused the plant to change its direction of growth.

270. Grassy Brick

Duration of Experiment: 2 weeks   Difficulty Level:

What you need:

Non-glazed porous brick

Grass seeds

Steel dish

Water

Bowl

What to do:

Step 1. Soak the brick in a bowl of water for a night.

Step 2. Put the brick in the steel dish the next day.

Step 3. Sprinkle grass seeds on the brick.

Step 4. Put the dish in a sunny spot. Fill half the dish with water.

Step 5. In a few days, you will see grass sprout!

What just happened? Though grass does not typically grow on brick since it gets no nutrition, plants are very adaptive and can survive in difficult conditions.

271. Seed Balls

Duration of Experiment: 5 days   Difficulty Level: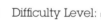

What you need:

Clay

Seeds

Soil

What to do:

Step 1. Shape the clay into a disc.

Step 2. Sprinkle the seeds and some soil on top of the clay.

Step 3. Fold the clay inwards and roll it so that the seeds and soil get incorporated in a ball. Mould it in the shape of a hedgehog.

Step 4. Keep it in your garden. Your hedgehog will start growing spines once it rains.

What just happened? The clay protects the seeds from wind and birds. The soil provides nutrients for them. Thus the seeds are safe till it rains and the clay soaks up the water, after which they begin to grow.

LIVE IT UP
Experiments on the human body

Your body is one of the most amazing scientific miracles. Did you know that in just one day, your heart beats 100,000 times? And that if you laid out all your blood vessels from end to end they would reach about 60,000 miles?

Scientists have figured out a lot about the way our body functions, but a lot still remains a mystery. Go ahead—discover more about yourself and your body in this section!

272. Eye See You

Duration of Experiment: ⏱ 10 mins.   Difficulty Level:

What you need:

Hand-held mirror   Chairs

What to do:

Step 1. Sit on the chair with the wall to your right.

Step 2. Ask a friend to sit a few feet away against the same wall.

Step 3. Hold the mirror against your nose with your left hand. You should be able to see the wall in the mirror.

Step 4. Adjust the mirror to see the reflection of the wall with your right eye and your friend's face with your left.

Step 5. Slowly, move your right hand in front of the white wall.

Step 6. At certain positions, your friend's face disappears!

💡 **What just happened?** The brain analyses and combines the messages it gets from each eye. When your eyes are seeing two such completely different pictures, the brain tries to put together an image that uses bits and pieces of both views.

273. Sniff it Out

Duration of Experiment: 15 mins.   Difficulty Level:

What you need:

Blindfold   Clothes belonging to   Chairs
                   different family members

What to do:

Step 1. Sit blindfolded on a chair.

Step 2. Ask your friend to hold out clothes belonging to you or your family members one at a time under your nose.

Step 3. Try to guess who the clothes belong to.

What just happened? The smell comes from pheromones that our body makes. This gives everyone a specific smell of their own. These smells are easy to recognise.

274. Watch Your Heartbeat

Duration of Experiment: 10 mins.   Difficulty Level:

What you need:

Flashlight   Bed

What to do:

Step 1. Jog till you feel breathless.

Step 2. Lie down on the bed. Put the flashlight on the left side of your chest.

Step 3. Lift your legs and point them towards a wall.

Step 4. Shine the light through your legs.

Step 5. You can see the shadow of your feet rise and fall as your heart beats!

What just happened? When you exercise, your muscles need more oxygen. This makes your heart pump faster. As it beats, it makes the flashlight rise and fall slightly, causing the change in shadow on the wall.

275. Strawberry DNA

Duration of Experiment: 1 hour.   Difficulty Level:

What you need:

Strawberry

5 ml isopropyl alcohol
(available at chemists)

Dishwashing liquid

¼ tsp. salt

Zip lock
bag

Plastic containers

Tweezers

90 ml water

Sieve

What to do:

Step 1. Put the isopropyl alcohol in the freezer.

Step 2. Mix the water, dishwashing liquid and salt in the plastic container.

Step 3. Put a strawberry in the zip lock bag. Remove as much air as you can to flatten it.

Step 4. Smash the strawberry with your hands till there are no chunks left.

Step 5. Pour this pulp and the solution you made earlier into another container through the sieve.

Step 6. Separate around 50-100 ml of this solution and add the isopropyl alcohol to it.

Step 7. The white layer on top of the rest of the solution is the DNA of the strawberry!

Step 8. You can remove this using tweezers.

What just happened? All living things contain DNA. The solution you made with the dishwashing liquid and the salt acts as an extraction solution. The soap dissolves the cell membranes. The salt breaks up protein chains that hold nucleic acid together. Finally, DNA is not soluble in isopropyl alcohol, making it easy to identify.

276. Fatty

Duration of Experiment: ⏱ **10** mins.   Difficulty Level: ▬ ▬ ▬

What you need:

Water

Fat (available at dairy stores)

Bucket

What to do:

Step 1. Make a small ball out of the fat.

Step 2. Coat one of your fingers with this.

Step 3. Dip this finger and another one in the bucket of ice cold water.

Step 4. The finger without the fat coating will start feeling colder first.

💡 **What just happened?** The fat forms a protective layer around your skin that does not let your body heat flow into the cold water. Whales, seals and other marine creatures often have such a layer of fat, called 'blubber', to keep them from freezing in the water.

277. Through Their Eyes

Duration of Experiment: ⏱ **10** mins.   Difficulty Level: ▬ ▬ ▬

What you need:

Shiny card paper

Scissors

What to do:

Step 1. Cut the shiny card paper in a rectangle that is 30 cm long and 9 cm wide.

Step 2. Put the card on your nose and bend the sides away from your face.

Step 3. Adjust the card so that whatever you are looking at is clearly in focus.

Step 4. You can see from either side of your head!

💡 **What just happened?** This is the way animals like horses and rabbits view the world. It is important for them to have 360° vision to escape predators.

278. Ghost of the Eaten Fish

Duration of Experiment: 10 mins.   Difficulty Level:

What you need:

2 white card papers   Red paper   Scissors   Glue   Black marker

What to do:

Step 1. Draw a fish on the red paper. Draw an eye with the marker.

Step 2. Cut it out and glue this onto the white card paper.

Step 3. On another white card paper, draw a fishbowl.

Step 4. Take the fish card to a bright area.

Step 5. Stare at the eye of the fish for 10-15 seconds.

Step 6. Now, quickly look at the card with the fishbowl. You can see the fish in the bowl, but with a blue-green tinge!

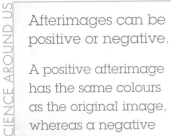

SCIENCE AROUND US

Afterimages can be positive or negative.

A positive afterimage has the same colours as the original image, whereas a negative afterimage has inverse colours (like the fish).

💡 **What just happened?** The ghostly fish is called an 'afterimage'. There are colour sensitive cells at the back of your eye. When you stare at the red fish for a long time, the 'red sensitive' cells get tired of responding to red. When you look at the blank card, your eyes respond to the green and blue light that the card is reflecting, but not the red, which is why you see a blue-green ghostly fish in the bowl.

279. All Taste, No Smell

Duration of Experiment: ⏱ 10 mins.   Difficulty Level:

What you need:

Raw potato   Apple   Peeler   Knife

What to do:

Step 1. Peel the apple and the potato.

Step 2. Cut an equal-sized slice from both.

Step 3. Close your eyes and mix up the potato and apple.

Step 4. Hold your nose and eat each piece.

They will taste the same.

💡 **What just happened?** Your nose and mouth are connected through the same airway, which means that you taste and smell foods at the same time.

280. Preserve a Spider Web

Duration of Experiment: ⏱ 60 mins.   Difficulty Level:

What you need:

Spider web   Spray glue   Gold spray paint   Black construction paper   Varnish   Cardboard box

What to do:

Step 1. Hold the box behind the spider web and spray it with the gold paint.

Step 2. Spray glue on the construction paper.

Step 3. While the glue is still wet, place the paper behind the spider web and carefully place the web onto the paper.

Step 4. Place the paper with the spider web on it at the bottom of the box. Coat the web with varnish.

💡 **What just happened?** The varnish helps preserve the web for months. Spider webs are important for spiders since they help them catch food.

281. Holy Hand

Duration of Experiment: ⏱ 5 mins.   Difficulty Level: ▬▬ ▬▬ ▬▬

What you need:

Newspapers

What to do:

Step 1. Take a square newspaper. Roll it into a tube.

Step 2. Hold the tube to your right eye.

Step 3. Raise your left palm in front of your left eye.

Step 4. Open both eyes and look straight ahead. You will see a hole in your hand!

💡 **What just happened?** Your brain receives conflicting images from both eyes and combines them to form the hole in your hand!

282. Right Eyed or Left?

Duration of Experiment: ⏱ 5 mins.   Difficulty Level: ▬▬ ▬▬ ▬▬

What you need:

Light switch

What to do:

Step 1. Stand 3 m away from the switch. Focus on it with both eyes.

Step 2. Hold up your thumb in front of your eyes till the object is blocked.

Step 3. Slowly close the left eye.

Step 4. If you cannot see the switch, then your left eye is more dominant.

Step 5. If you can see the switch, then your right eye is more dominant.

💡 **What just happened?** Just like you are right or left-handed, similarly you prefer inputs from one eye over the other too. This is one way of finding out which of your eyes is dominant.

283. Cage the Bird

Duration of Experiment: 10 mins.   Difficulty Level:

What you need:

Pencil   2 white card papers   Glue

What to do:

Step 1. Draw a cage on one card paper and a bird on the other.

Step 2. Stick both papers with the pencil in the middle.

Step 3. Hold the pencil between your hands and roll it quickly to cage the bird.

What just happened? The eye retains images for about $\frac{1}{16}$th of a second. This is called 'persistence of vision'. When your eye sees the bird and the cage in rapid succession, both pictures get merged and it looks like the bird is in the cage.

284. Balancing Act

Duration of Experiment: 10 mins.   Difficulty Level:

What you need:

Pencil   Paper   Stop watch

What to do:

Step 1. Ask a friend to record the timings on a piece of paper as you do the following activities.

Step 2. First, stand on each leg with your eyes open.

Step 3. Next, close your eyes and try to stand on each leg.

Step 4. Compare the timings. You will be able to balance longer when your eyes are open compared to when they are shut.

What just happened? In order to maintain our balance, we use a lot of reference points in our surrounding. We tend to lose our balance without these reference points.

285. Eye Eye Captain

Duration of Experiment: 10 mins.　Difficulty Level:

What you need:

Cardboard egg carton　　Scissors　　Skewer

What to do:

Step 1. Cut out two egg holders from the carton.

Step 2. Make a hole at the bottom of each holder with the skewer, a little away from the centre.

Step 3. Look through the egg holder. You can see in two different directions!

What just happened? This is how chameleons and some other reptiles view the world. They can see in two different directions.

286. Fingerprints

Duration of Experiment: 20 mins.　Difficulty Level: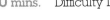

What you need:

Pencil　　Paper　　　Tape　　Magnifying glass

What to do:

Step 1. Use the pencil to colour on the paper till you have a thin layer of graphite.

Step 2. Rub each of your fingers across the graphite.

Step 3. Tear out some tape and stick it across your fingers.

Step 4. Remove the tape and stick it on the white paper.

Step 5. Examine each of the prints with a magnifying glass.

What just happened? All your fingerprints are identical. The projections are made five months before a baby is even born! And these never change.

287. Tasty!

Duration of Experiment: 10 mins.   Difficulty Level: ▬ ▬ ▬

What you need:

Food colouring

Cotton ball

Paper

Punch

Mirror

What to do:

Step 1. Dip the cotton ball in food colouring and swipe it across your tongue.

Step 2. Punch a hole in the paper and put it on your tongue.

Step 3. Look in a mirror and count the number of bumps you can see in the hole. If there are more than 25, you are a super taster!

What just happened? The tiny bumps on your tongue are your taste buds. There are four types of taste buds—bitter, sour, salty and sweet. The more taste buds you have, the better your sense of taste.

288. Pulsating

Duration of Experiment: 10 mins.   Difficulty Level: ▬ ▬ ▬

What you need:

Soft board pin with large, slightly round bottom

Matchstick

What to do:

Step 1. Stick the pin into the matchstick such that it can balance on a flat surface.

Step 2. Place this on the part of your wrist where the pulse feels strongest.

Step 3. You can see the match move backward and forward with each heartbeat!

What just happened? What you can see and count is your pulse. A normal pulse rate for an adult is anywhere between 60 and 100 per minute.

289. Flip it

Duration of Experiment: ⏱ 1 hour   Difficulty Level: ▬▬ ▬ ▬

What you need:

Paper   Stapler   Pencil   Scissors

What to do:

Step 1. Cut the paper to 20–30 rectangles around 15 cm x 20 cm.

Step 2. Staple them on one side.

Step 3. Start by drawing something on the last page. (E.g. A person with his hand down.)

Step 4. On the second last page, draw the exact same thing, but with a slight variation. (E.g. The person with his hand slightly raised.)

Step 5. Change the drawing a little more on the third last page. (E.g. Raise the hand even more.)

Step 6. Keep going till you eventually reach the first page.

Step 7. Now flip the pages to enjoy the illusion of motion!

💡 **What just happened?** The drawing looks like it is moving because every picture remains in the mind for a split second after it has actually disappeared. This is called 'persistence of vision'. So, when you flip them all quickly, because the previous picture is still in your mind, it merges with the current picture and gives the illusion of motion.

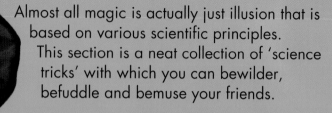

GOT YOU!
Science tricks and pranks

Almost all magic is actually just illusion that is based on various scientific principles.
This section is a neat collection of 'science tricks' with which you can bewilder, befuddle and bemuse your friends.

Confuse them with rubber bones, disappearing ink, invisible ink, vanishing water, paper loop, and more!

290. Rubber Bones

Duration of Experiment: ⏱ **3 days**   Difficulty Level: ▬ ▬ ▬

What you need:

Chicken bones

Jar

Cooking vinegar

What to do:

Step 1. Fill the jar with vinegar and submerge the chicken bones in it.

Step 2. Close the jar and set it aside for three days.

Step 3. Remove the bone after three days.

Step 4. It will be rubbery—not at all like the bone that you put in the jar!

💡 **What just happened?** The acetic acid in the vinegar dissolved all the calcium in the bone. Calcium is what makes bones hard. Once that was gone, your bone was transformed into a rather malleable substance.

291. Good Juice, Bad Juice

Duration of Experiment: **30** mins.   Difficulty Level:

What you need:

Glasses

Safety goggles

Rubber gloves

½ tsp. cooking vinegar

Water

1 tsp. red grape juice

⅛ tsp. ammonia (available at super-markets and grocery stores)

What to do:

Step 1. Wear the safety goggles and rubber gloves.

Step 2. In the first glass, add water and grape juice.

Step 3. In the second, add ammonia.

Step 4. In the third, add vinegar.

Step 5. Gather an audience.

Step 6. Start off with the first glass, saying that it is good juice.

Step 7. Pour it into the second glass. The juice will turn green. Say that the good juice has now turned bad.

Step 8. Finally, ask the audience to pray real hard for the juice to turn good again.

Step 9. Pour this solution into the last glass, and voila! The liquid returns to its original colour!

> ! Do not try to drink ANY of the solutions created during this experiment. Use gloves while conducting the experiment, as ammonia can cause tissue damage if it comes in contact with your skin.

What just happened? When you poured the grape juice into the ammonia, it created an alkaline solution which was green in colour. In the third glass, the acidic vinegar neutralises the alkaline solution, returning it to its original colour.

292. Disappearing Ink

Duration of Experiment: 15 mins. Difficulty Level: ▬ ▬ ▬

What you need:

Starch   Cup   Water   Iodine   Paper   Ear bud

What to do:

Step 1. Mix the water, iodine and starch in the cup until it turns into a smooth, thin paste.

Step 2. Dip the ear bud into this mixture and write with it on the paper.

Step 3. Once it dries, you can wipe it off with your hand. It disappears!

💡 **What just happened?** The iodine gives the ink its colour. When it is still wet, the water helps hold the ink and paper together. Once it dries, it is easy to wipe it off.

293. Paper Loop

Duration of Experiment: 🕐 10 mins. Difficulty Level: ▬ ▬ ▬

What you need:

Scissors   7 cm x 12 cm cardpaper

What to do:

Step 1. Fold the card lengthwise in half.

Step 2. Make 13 cuts width-wise.

Step 3. First cut from the edges toward the folded centre, then turn the paper around and cut from the centre towards the edge.

Step 4. Now, carefully open out the paper and cut along the fold. Don't cut the two sections at the edge.

Step 5. Shake the paper a little. You'll have a loop that goes over your head!

💡 **What just happened?** The secret to this trick comes from a branch of mathematics called 'topology'. It teaches that figures can be stretched without changing their area.

294. Invisible Ink

Duration of Experiment: ⏱ 20 mins.   Difficulty Level: ▬ ▬ ▬

What you need:

½ lemon   Water   Bowl   Ear bud   White paper   Iron

What to do:

Step 1. Squeeze the lemon into the bowl.
Add a few drops of water to it.

Step 2. Mix the water and lemon juice.

Step 3. Dip one end of your ear bud into the solution.

Step 4. Write a message on the white paper.

Step 5. To read the secret message, run a hot iron over it.

💡 **What just happened?** Lemon juice oxidises and turns brown when heated. Diluting it makes it hard to notice till it is heated!

295. Vanishing Water

Duration of Experiment: ⏱ 10 mins.   Difficulty Level: ▬ ▬ ▬

What you need:

Opaque mug   1 tbsp. sodium polyacrylate (available in lab supply stores and online)   Water

What to do:

Step 1. Challenge a friend that you can make water disappear.

Step 2. Before you begin, put the sodium polyacrylate in the mug.

Step 3. Show your friend that you are pouring water into the mug.

Step 4. In a few minutes, turn the cup over. Nothing pours out!

💡 **What just happened?** The polyacrylate absorbs the water and turns into a gel. Polyacrylate has the ability to absorb as much as 200 to 300 times its mass in water.

296. Stink it Up

Duration of Experiment: **4 days**   Difficulty Level:

What you need:

Scissors   Jar   20 strike-anywhere matchsticks   2 tbsp. household ammonia (available at grocery stores and supermarkets)

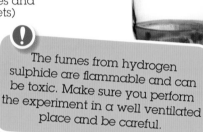

What to do:

Step 1. Cut the heads of the matchsticks.

Step 2. Put them in the jar and add the ammonia.

Step 3. Close the jar and swirl the contents around.

Step 4. Wait for four days and then open the jar to unleash the stench!

 The fumes from hydrogen sulphide are flammable and can be toxic. Make sure you perform the experiment in a well ventilated place and be careful.

What just happened? The matchstick heads are made out of phosphorus sulphide. The phosphorus sulphide and ammonia react to form a nasty smelling substance called ammonium sulphide.

297. Magic Paper

Duration of Experiment: **15 mins.**   Difficulty Level:

What you need:

Tongs   Alcohol (90%)   Candle   Water   Paper

What to do:

Step 1. Make a solution of 50% alcohol and 50% water.

Step 2. Soak the paper in this solution till it is completely wet.

Step 3. Hold the paper with the tongs.

Step 4. Light the paper and wait till the flame dies.

What just happened? When the paper is soaked in alcohol-water solution, the alcohol coats the outside of the material and only the alcohol burns when it is lit. The water does not evaporate, so the paper remains wet and can't catch fire.

HIGH AND DRY
Experiments with water

We all know that water covers a majority of the Earth's surface. We also know how important water is for our survival. In fact, 70% of our body is made up of water.

One of the properties of water, that makes it very interesting to study, is known as surface tension. Surface tension is the ability of water to form a thin, skin-like membrane over its surface (like the layer that forms on top of a thick soup).

298. Glow in the Dark Water

Duration of Experiment: ○ 15 mins.   Difficulty Level: ▬ ▬ ▬

What you need:

Highlighter

Water

Black light
(available at hardware stores or online)

What to do:

Step 1. Remove the felt from the highlighter and soak it in water for a few minutes.

Step 2. Go to a dark room and turn on the black light near the water.

Step 3. The water will 'glow'.

💡 **What just happened?** The dye from the highlighter pens contain phosphors that turn UV light (light we can't see) into visible light (light we can see). That's why the water glows in the dark when you shine a black light on it.

299. Coloured Ice

Duration of Experiment: ⏱ **30** mins.   Difficulty Level: ▬ ▬ ▬

What you need:

Containers   Large tray   Watercolours   Water   Salt

What to do:

Step 1. Fill different sized containers with water and put them in the freezer overnight.

Step 2. The next day, take the ice out in a large tray.

Step 3. Put some salt on the ice. Wait for a few minutes.

Step 4. On top of the ice blocks, put a few drops of water colour.

Step 5. The colour runs down the ice in rivulets, creating a fantastic display of colour!

💡 **What just happened?** Salt lowers the freezing point of water. So, when you add it to ice it melts at the points where the salt comes in contact with the ice. The colour runs down the ravines caused in these blocks by the salt.

300. Tornado in a Bottle

Duration of Experiment: 10 mins.   Difficulty Level:

What you need:

Glitter

Glass jar

Water

Dishwashing liquid

What to do:

Step 1. Fill $\frac{3}{4}^{th}$ of the glass jar with water.

Step 2. Add a few drops of dishwashing liquid and some glitter.

Step 3. Put the cap on tightly.

Step 4. Quickly spin the bottle in a circular motion for a few seconds.

Step 5. Stop and look inside to see if you can see a mini tornado forming in the water.

What just happened? Spinning the bottle in a circular motion creates a water vortex that looks like a mini tornado because of a force called the 'centripetal' force.

301. Moving Molecules

Duration of Experiment: 10 mins.   Difficulty Level:

What you need:

Hot water

Cold water

Glasses

Food colouring

Eye dropper

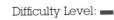

What to do:

Step 1. Fill one glass with hot water and the other with cold water.

Step 2. Put one drop of food colouring into both glasses at the same time.

Step 3. Watch as the food colouring spreads faster through the hot water than the cold.

What just happened? The molecules in the hot water move at a faster rate, spreading the food colouring faster than the cold water molecules which move slower.

302. Wet Pepper

Duration of Experiment: ⏱ 10 mins.　Difficulty Level: ▬ ▬ ▬

What you need:

Pepper　　　Water　　　Dishwashing liquid　　Bowl

What to do:

Step 1. Fill the bowl with water.

Step 2. Shake some pepper onto the surface of the water.

Step 3. Dip a finger in. Nothing spectacular happens.

Step 4. Put a little dishwashing liquid on your finger and dip your finger in the water again.

Step 5. Watch the pepper race to the edge of the bowl.

💡 **What just happened?** Coating your finger with soap when you dip it in the water reduces the surface tension of the water. Therefore, the pepper spreads out.

303. Dry Hands

Duration of Experiment: ⏱ 10 mins.　Difficulty Level: ▬ ▬ ▬

What you need:

Talcum powder　　Bowl　　　Water　　　Coin

What to do:

Step 1. Drop a coin into the bowl of water.

Step 2. Try to remove it with your hand without wetting your hand. Quite impossible, isn't it?

Step 3. Sprinkle a layer of talcum powder on the surface of the water.

Step 4. You can now put your hand in and retrieve the coin without wetting your hand!

💡 **What just happened?** As soon as you put your hand in the water, it gets covered with the powder, which makes your hand waterproof.

304. Speedy Matchsticks

Duration of Experiment: ⏱ 10 mins.   Difficulty Level: ▬▬ ▬▬ ▬▬

What you need:

Water   Bowl   Dishwashing liquid   Matchsticks

What to do:

Step 1. Fill the bowl with water and place a few matchsticks on the surface.

Step 2. Put a drop of dishwashing liquid in the bowl and watch the matchsticks race across the surface!

💡 **What just happened?** Soap reduces the surface tension of water, pushing the matchsticks away. The water molecules on the surface of water stick to each other, forming a sort of layer (like the type that forms on top of a soup). This is known as 'surface tension'.

305. Rainy

Duration of Experiment: ⏱ 30 mins.   Difficulty Level: ▬▬ ▬▬ ▬▬

What you need:

Glass mug   Electric kettle

What to do:

Step 1. Put the mug in the fridge for 10 minutes.

Step 2. Boil some water in the kettle.

Step 3. Hold the cold mug over the stream of hot air coming out of the kettle and watch water droplets form!

💡 **What just happened?** When water is heated, it forms vapour and rises. When it comes in contact with something cold, it forms water droplets again.

306. Rain Gauge

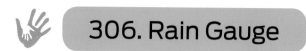

Duration of Experiment: ⏱ **30** mins.   Difficulty Level: ▬ ▬▬ ▬▬

What you need:

Plastic bottle   Stones or pebbles   Sticky tape   Marker   Ruler   Water   Knife

What to do:

Step 1. Cut off the top of the bottle.

Step 2. Place some stones at the bottom of the bottle.

Step 3. Turn the top upside down and tape it to the bottle.

Step 4. Use the ruler and marker to make a scale on the bottle.

Step 5. Pour water into the bottle till it reaches the lowest mark on the scale.

Step 6. Now put it outdoors when it starts raining.

Measure the rising water level.

💡 **What just happened?** The rain falls on top of the gauge and collects at the bottom, where it can be measured easily. Measure the rainfall in your gauge every time it rains. Then, try to identify what type of shower it was – short or long, heavy or light.

307. Expanding Ice

Duration of Experiment: 2 hours   Difficulty Level:

What you need:

Plastic bottle   Water   Aluminium foil   Dishwashing liquid   Glitter

What to do:

Step 1. Fill the bottle with water to the brim.

Step 2. Add a few drops of dishwashing liquid and some glitter.

Step 3. Create a 'cap' out of the foil and place it on top of the bottle. Put the bottle in the freezer.

Step 4. Check on your bottle two hours later. You will notice that the ice has 'pushed' the aluminium up.

What just happened? Most substances expand when heated and contract when cooled. However, water is an exception to this rule. It expands when cooled.

308. Waterproof Bag

Duration of Experiment:  10 mins.   Difficulty Level:

What you need:

Sharp pencils   Zip lock bag   Water

What to do:

Step 1. Fill half the zip lock bag with water and seal it.

Step 2. Push the pencils through the bag.

Step 3. Push as many pencils as you like, the water will not leak out of the bag!

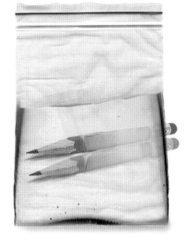

What just happened? Plastic is a polymer. This means that it is made up of small, chain like molecules. These molecules wrap themselves around the pencil, sealing it.

309. Sweet as Sugar

Duration of Experiment: ⏱ 10 mins.   Difficulty Level: ▬▬ ▬ ▬

What you need:

Matchsticks   Soap   Water   Sugar   Bowl

What to do:

Step 1. Arrange the matchsticks in a circle in a bowl of water.

Step 2. Touch the water in the centre with a piece of soap.

Step 3. The matchsticks drift towards the edge of the bowl.

Step 4. Replace the soap with a lump of sugar. The matches move towards the centre.

💡 **What just happened?** Sugar absorbs a little bit of water, creating an inward current. The soap reduces the surface tension of water, pushing the matchsticks away.

310. Spilt Oil

Duration of Experiment: ⏱ 15 mins.   Difficulty Level: ▬ ▬ ▬ ▬

What you need:

Tub   Water   Food colouring   Oil   Rubber bath toy

What to do:

Step 1. Fill half the tub with water.

Step 2. Add blue food colouring.

Step 3. Put the small toy in the tub.

Step 4. Pour the cooking oil into the tub. Swirl the mixture to create waves.

Step 5. Notice how the oil and water don't mix, but your toy gets coated with oil.

💡 **What just happened?** Oil is not as dense as water and doesn't mix with it. This is exactly what happens during oil spills. Marine life finds it difficult to breathe.

311. Wind in a Bowl

Duration of Experiment: ⏱ 1 hour   Difficulty Level: ▬ ▬ ▬

What you need:

Water   Bowl   Food colouring   Ice tray

What to do:

Step 1. Fill the ice tray with water. Put different food colouring in each cube. Put it in the freezer.

Step 2. Fill the bowl with cold water.

Step 3. Put the ice cubes in the bowl.

Step 4. You will see coloured water around the sides of the ice cube.

💡 **What just happened?** The water that melts from the ice is colder than the water in the bowl. This means that it is denser than the rest of the water. So, it sinks.

312. Float or Sink?

Duration of Experiment: ⏱ 5 mins.   Difficulty Level: ▬ ▬ ▬

What you need:

Limes and lemons of about the same size   Bowl   Water

What to do:

Step 1. In a bowl of water, drop the limes and the lemons.

Step 2. You will notice that the lemons float but the limes don't!

💡 **What just happened?** Even though the lime and the lemon are exactly the same in terms of their weight and size, limes are denser than lemons. This is why the lemon floats and the lime sinks.

313. The Science of Bubbles

Duration of Experiment: 10 mins.   Difficulty Level:

What you need:

Clay   4 tbsp. glycerine   4½ cups water   Toothpicks   Dishwashing liquid

What to do:

Step 1. Mix the dishwashing liquid, water and glycerine to form bubble liquid.

Step 2. Use the clay and toothpicks to make a 3D bubble wand.

Step 3. You can make a cube or a pyramid as shown.

Step 4. Dip the entire wand in the bubble mix and observe the funny shapes the bubbles make BEFORE you blow through them.

💡 **What just happened?** A bubble always tries to form a shape with minimal surface area. In free air, it is always a sphere. But with your special wands, you get an unexpected shape!

314. Frozen Bubbles

Duration of Experiment: 30 mins.   Difficulty Level:

What you need:

½ cup powdered soap   ½ cup sugar   Water   Bubble wand

What to do:

Step 1. Mix the powdered soap and sugar in three cups of water.

Step 2. Blow a bubble carefully in the freezer with the bubble wand.

Step 3. The bubble will soon freeze into a fragile crystal ball.

💡 **What just happened?** A majority of the bubble solution is water. When you put it in the freezer, the water freezes to form little icicles on the balloon surface.

315. Crystallise

Duration of Experiment: 3 hours   Difficulty Level:

What you need:

Scissors   Black chart paper   Pan   ¼ cup water   1 tbsp. epsom salt
(available at a pharmacy)

What to do:

Step 1. Cut the black paper so that it lines the bottom of the pan.

Step 2. Mix the epsom salt and the water.

Step 3. Pour the salty water into the pan.

Step 4. Put the pan out in the Sun.

Step 5. After a few hours, you will see lots of crystal spikes on the paper!

What just happened? The salt dissolves in the water when you first mix it. In the Sun, the water evaporates, leaving the crystals behind.

316. Soap-powered Boat

Duration of Experiment: 15 mins.   Difficulty Level:

What you need:

Dishwashing   Visiting card   Water   Tray   Scissors
liquid

What to do:

Step 1: Cut the card in the shape of a boat base.

Step 2: Using the scissors, make a little groove in the card at the back of the boat.

Step 3: Fill the tray with water and place the boat gently on the water, so that it floats.

Step 4: Place a drop of dishwashing liquid in the groove. Watch your boat go!

What just happened? You break the surface tension of water by adding a drop of dishwashing liquid. This force is enough to propel the boat.

317. Fireworks in a Glass

Duration of Experiment: ⏱ 15 mins.   Difficulty Level: ▬▬ ▬▬ ▬▬

What you need:

Fork

2 tbsp. oil

Plastic container

Water

2 drops food colouring

Tall, transparent glass

What to do:

Step 1. Fill the glass with water. Pour the oil in the plastic container.

Step 2. Add the food colouring to the oil and mix it lightly with the fork.

Step 3. Pour the oil and colour into the glass and watch as the food colouring sinks to the bottom of the glass, expanding outwards as it falls, resembling fireworks.

💡 **What just happened?** Since oil is less dense than water, it floats on top of the glass. As the coloured drops sink to the bottom, they mix with the water and diffuse outward.

318. Spin the Bottle

Duration of Experiment: ⏱ 30 mins.   Difficulty Level: ▬▬ ▬▬ ▬▬

What you need:

Scissors

Bottle

Straw

Scotch tape

Water

Knife

Strings

What to do:

Step 1. Cut the top of the bottle with the knife.

Step 2. Make six holes in the base of the bottle with the scissorss.

Step 3. Cut the straw into six pieces and insert them into the bottle. Secure them with tape.

Step 4. Make three holes at the top of the bottle and tie three strings to this.

Step 5. Go outdoors and pour a jug of water into the bottle. Watch it spin!

💡 **What just happened?** The energy from the water pouring out of the holes is enough to get the bottle going.

319. Floating Paper Clip

Duration of Experiment: ⏱ 5 mins.   Difficulty Level: ▬▬ ▬▬ ▬▬

What you need:

1 transparent glass of water

1 clean tissue

1 clean paper clip

What to do:

Step 1. Gently drop a clean piece of tissue onto the surface of the water.

Step 2. Carefully place the paper clip on the tissue. Your hands shouldn't touch either the tissue or the water.

Step 3. Poke the tissue with a pencil and make sure that it sinks alone.

Step 4. The paperclip will continue floating on the surface.

💡 **What just happened?** The paperclip did not sink due to surface tension. Under certain conditions, surface tension helps to bind the molecules of water tightly together. This creates a platform for light weighted objects and, therefore, they don't sink.

320. Floating Ball

Duration of Experiment: ⏱ 30 mins.   Difficulty Level: ▬▬ ▬▬ ▬▬

What you need:

Ping-pong ball

Plastic glass

Water

What to do:

Step 1. Fill half the glass with water.

Step 2. Try to get the ping-pong ball to float right in the middle of the glass. Tough, right?

Step 3. Now, fill the glass all the way to the top till it is almost overflowing. Voila! It is much easier to get the ping-pong ball to remain in the centre.

💡 **What just happened?** Surface tension pulls the ball towards the side when the glass is only half full, but forms a membrane for the ball to balance on when it is brimming.

SHOCKING
Experiments on the principle of static

If you have ever touched someone or something on a dry winter morning and felt a sudden shock or current pass through, you have experienced static electricity.

Static electricity is created when small negatively charged particles (called electrons) jump from one object to another. Static is extremely fun and interesting to experiment with.

321. Bending Water

Duration of Experiment: ⏱ **10** mins. Difficulty Level: ▬ ▬▬ ▬▬

What you need:

Narrow stream of water from a tap

Plastic comb

What to do:

Step 1. Turn on the water so it falls from the tap in a narrow stream.

Step 2. Run the comb through your hair around 10 times.

Step 3. Slowly, move the comb towards the water (without touching it).

Step 4. You will see the water 'bend'.

💡 **What just happened?** The static electricity you built up by combing your hair attracts the stream of water, bending it towards or away from the comb!

322. Can Follower

Duration of Experiment: 🕐 10 mins.   Difficulty Level: ▬ ▬ ▬

What you need:

Inflated balloon   Aluminium can   Woollen fabric

What to do:

Step 1. Rub the balloon against the woollen fabric.

Step 2. Put the aluminium can on its side on a table.

Step 3. Hold the balloon close to the can and watch as the can rolls towards it.

Step 4. Slowly use the balloon to lead the can.

💡 **What just happened?** Rubbing the balloon against the woollen fabric creates static electricity. This involves negatively charged particles (electrons) moving from the wool to the balloon. The aluminium can, which is neutral, is drawn to the negatively charged balloon.

323. Static Magic

Duration of Experiment: 🕐 30 mins.   Difficulty Level: ▬ ▬ ▬

What you need:

Woollen fabric   Plastic straw   Styrofoam ball

What to do:

Step 1. Wrap the piece of fabric around the plastic straw and rub it 20 times.

Step 2. Place the now magic straw above the foam ball and watch the ball mysteriously jump up to the straw.

💡 **What just happened?** When the straw is rubbed with the fabric it gets charged. This gives it the power to attract things like the styrofoam ball.

324. Shock Yourself

Duration of Experiment: **20** mins.   Difficulty Level:

What you need:

Glass slab   Piece of fur   Tap

What to do:

Step 1. On a dry day, place the glass slab on the floor.

Step 2. Stand on the slab. Have your friend rub your back with the fur several times.

Step 3. Now slowly bring your finger close to a water tap. See the spark fly. You have just given yourself a shock!

What just happened? You acted as a conductor of electricity when your back was rubbed. The glass you were standing on, however, kept you insulated and prevented the harmful effects of the shock.

325. The Tissue Dance

Duration of Experiment: **20** mins.   Difficulty Level: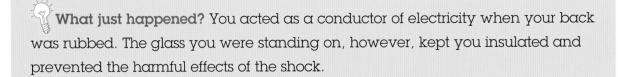

What you need:

Glass pane   Two thick books   Woollen fabric   Tissue paper

What to do:

Step 1. Place the glass pane across two thick books.

Step 2. Tear the tissue into small pieces and put it under the glass.

Step 3. Rub the glass with the wool.

Step 4. Watch the tissue jump up and dance.

What just happened? Rubbing the glass produced static electricity, to which the tissue pieces were attracted.

326. Jumping Pepper

Duration of Experiment: ⏱ 10 mins.   Difficulty Level: ▬▬ ▬▬ ▬▬

What you need:

Pepper

Plastic box

Woollen fabric

What to do:

Step 1. Sprinkle a thin layer of pepper into a small plastic box.

Step 2. Shut the box and rub the lid with the woollen fabric.

Step 3. See the pepper jump up and stick to the lid.

💡 **What just happened?** Rubbing the lid of the box caused a buildup of static electricity to which the pepper was attracted.

327. Salt and Pepper Separation

Duration of Experiment: ⏱ 10 mins.   Difficulty Level: ▬▬ ▬▬ ▬▬

What you need:

Salt

Pepper

Plastic spoon

Woollen fabric

What to do:

Step 1. Sprinkle a little salt and pepper on a flat surface and mix them up.

Step 2. Rub a plastic spoon with the wool.

Step 3. Hold the spoon above the salt and pepper, and bring it down slowly.

Step 4. The pepper particles will jump up and stick to the spoon.

💡 **What just happened?** When you charge the spoon, the salt and pepper become attracted to it. However, because pepper is lighter than salt, it jumps up before the salt.

328. Swinging Cereal

Duration of Experiment: ⏱ 10 mins.   Difficulty Level: ▬ ▬ ▬ ▬ ▬ ▬

What you need:

Comb   Thread   Small pieces of dry cereal   Doorknob

What to do:

Step 1. Tie a piece of cereal to one end of a string.

Step 2. Hang the string from a metal doorknob.

Step 3. Comb your hair briskly with a dry comb around 20 times.

Step 4. Now bring the comb close to the cereal. It will swing to touch the comb.

Step 5. Wait for a few seconds till it jumps away.

Step 6. Now every time you try to touch it, it will move away.

Step 7. You can control the cereal in this way, just like a remote control car!

SCIENCE AROUND US

Photocopy machines use static electricity

It's true! In copy machines more ink gets attracted to darker areas because of static. Copy machines use the charge to apply ink only in the areas where the paper to be copied is darker and not where the paper is white.

💡 **What just happened?** When you combed your hair, the comb got negatively charged. Being neutral, the cereal jumped to the comb. As soon as this happened, negative electrons got transferred from the comb to the cereal. Once this happened, both objects had a negative charge and repelled each other.

329. Combing Sparks

Duration of Experiment: ⏱ **10** mins.   Difficulty Level: ▬ ▬ ▬

What you need:

Comb   Metal doorknob

What to do:

Step 1. On a dry day, comb your hair briskly to 'charge' the comb.

Step 2. Hold the end of the comb about half a centimetre above the doorknob in a dark room.

Step 3. You will see a tiny spark jump across.

💡 **What just happened?** Combing your hair creates static electricity and creates a charge, which gives rise to the sparks.

330. Create Static

Duration of Experiment: ⏱ **15** mins.   Difficulty Level: ▬ ▬ ▬

What you need:

Phonograph record   Woollen fabric   Wooden ruler   Metal jar cover   Nail

What to do:

Step 1. Nail the metal cover to the ruler.

Step 2. Rub the record with the wool for 15 seconds.

Step 3. Holding the ruler, touch the metal cover to the record.

Step 4. Touch the metal cover and the record simultaneously with your free hand.

Step 5. You will observe a spark jump.

💡 **What just happened?** Rubbing the record created a charge in the record. This electric charge gave off the spark when you touched it.

331. Static Flower

Duration of Experiment: ⏱ 15 mins.   Difficulty Level: ▬ ■ ▤

What you need:

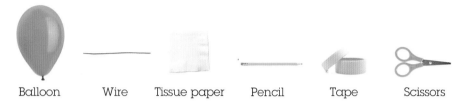

Balloon   Wire   Tissue paper   Pencil   Tape   Scissors

What to do:

Step 1. Make small loops at both ends of the wire.

Step 2. Cut thin strips out of the tissue paper and push them in through one end such that equal lengths of paper stick out.

Step 3. Tape the pencil to the middle of the wire to make a handle.

Step 4. Blow up the balloon and rub it in your hair to create static.

Step 5. Hold the pencil in your hand and touch the balloon to the free end of the wire.

Step 6. Watch the 'petals' unfold.

SCIENCE AROUND US

Static is used to paint cars.

To make sure a car's paint is uniform and that it will resist the high speeds, it is applied with a static charge. The metal body of the car is submerged in a substance that charges it positively and the paint is charged negatively with the paint sprayer.

💡 **What just happened?** The balloon transfers its charge through the wire to the paper petals. Having the same charge, the petals repel each other and stick out in different directions.

332. Dancing Dolls

Duration of Experiment: ⏱ 15 mins.   Difficulty Level: ▬ ▬ ▬

What you need:

Tissue paper   Scissors   Table   Flannel cloth   Two thick books   Glass pane

What to do:

Step 1. Cut out two figures from
the tissue paper in the shape of dolls.
Step 2. Put the two books on a table
and put the glass pane on top of it.

Step 3. Put the two dolls below the glass between the two books.
Step 4. Rub the glass with the flannel cloth and watch your dolls dance.

💡 **What just happened?** The charged glass attracts the uncharged dolls, so they stand up. When they touch the glass, they become charged and are repelled. So, they lay back down.

333. Merry Go Round

Duration of Experiment: ⏱ 15 mins.   Difficulty Level: ▬ ▬ ▬

What you need:

Glass   Cork   Woollen fabric   Paper   Needle   Scissors

What to do:

Step 1. Cut out a cross from the paper.
Step 2. Push a needle into the cork. Balance the cross on
top of the needle. Turn the glass over this.
Step 3. Rub the glass with the woollen fabric and see the cross rotate.

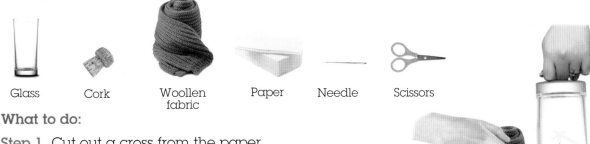

💡 **What just happened?** By rubbing the glass, you created a negative charge. Repelled by this, the paper rotates.

334. Electrical Paper Hanging

Duration of Experiment: 15 mins.   Difficulty Level: ▬▬ ▬▬ ▬▬

What you need:

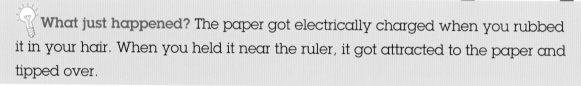

| Paper | Long wooden ruler | Chair |

What to do:

Step 1. Balance the ruler on the top of the chair.

Step 2. Rub the paper in your hair and then hold the paper just below the ruler.

Step 3. The ruler tips over without you touching it.

What just happened? The paper got electrically charged when you rubbed it in your hair. When you held it near the ruler, it got attracted to the paper and tipped over.

335. Electric Pendulum

Duration of Experiment: 15 mins.   Difficulty Level: ▬▬ ▬▬ ▬▬

What you need:

| Glass bottle | Corks | String | Comb | Copper wire |

What to do:

Step 1. Shut the bottle with the cork.

Step 2. Stick the wire into the cork, parallel to the ground.

Step 3. Tie the string to the end of the wire.

Step 4. Tie a small piece of cork to the bottom of the string.

Step 5. Run the comb through your hair and hold it close to the cork. Enjoy your swinging pendulum.

What just happened? The comb got electrically charged when you combed your hair and attracted the small cork.

336. Electroscope

Duration of Experiment: ⏱ 15 mins.   Difficulty Level: ▬ ▬ ▬

What you need:

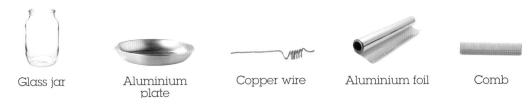

Glass jar   Aluminium   Copper wire   Aluminium foil   Comb
                    plate

What to do:

Step 1. Bend the copper wire in a 'Z' shape.

Step 2. Fold the foil and hang it on the bottom of the wire.

Step 3. Leave the top horizontal part over the top of the jar.

Step 4. Put the aluminium plate on top to hold it in place.

Step 5. Run the comb through your hair and bring it close to the jar.

Step 6. You will see the two strips of aluminium spring apart.

💡 **What just happened?** When you bring the comb close to the aluminium foil, it becomes charged. Since like charges repel, the aluminium foil leaves repel each other.

337. Bubble Ballet

Duration of Experiment: 🕐 15 mins.   Difficulty Level:

What you need:

Comb   Bubble liquid   Wire   Stool

What to do:

Step 1. Twist the wire to form the shape of a bubble blower.

Step 2. Blow some bubbles onto a flat surface, like a stool.

Step 3. Run the comb through your hair and hold it close to some bubbles.

Step 4. The bubbles, attracted to the comb, form a funny shape.

💡 **What just happened?** The charged comb attracts the bubbles towards it, making them change their shape.

338. Magic Wand

Duration of Experiment: 🕐 15 mins.   Difficulty Level:

What you need:

Pencil   PVC pipe   Styrofoam sheets   Woollen fabric   Scissors   Tape

What to do:

Step 1. Cut out a strip from the styrofoam sheet.

Step 2. Tape the ends together to make a ring.

Step 3. Rub the woollen fabric on the ring.

Step 4. Tape the pencil to the end of the PVC pipe.

Step 5. Use the pencil and pipe to toss the ring up in the air.

Step 6. Quickly position the pipe under the ring to make it levitate!

💡 **What just happened?** The static charge in the pipe repelled the charge in the styrofoam ring.

339. Genie in a Bottle

Duration of Experiment: ⏱ 15 mins.　Difficulty Level: ▬ ▬ ▬

What you need:

Plastic bottle　　Styrofoam beads

What to do:

Step 1. Fill half the bottle with the styrofoam beads.

Step 2. Rub the bottle to your hair.

Step 3. Run your hand over the bottle to see the beads jumping to avoid your finger.

💡 **What just happened?** When you rubbed the bottle to your hair, it created an electric charge. This charge got transferred to the styrofoam. Your hand, too, has a similar charge, which causes the styrofoam to get repelled by your hand.

340. Holy Balloon!

Duration of Experiment: ⏱ 15 mins.　Difficulty Level: ▬ ▬ ▬

What you need:

Scissors　　Woollen fabric　　Plastic bag　　Balloon

What to do:

Step 1. Cut out a strip from the open end of the plastic bag.

Step 2. Blow the balloon and tie it up.

Step 3. Rub the balloon with the woollen fabric for 45 seconds.

Step 4. Flatten the plastic ring and rub it with the same woollen fabric.

Step 5. Leave the band about one foot over the balloon and release it.

The ring floats over the balloon, giving it a halo!

💡 **What just happened?** Rubbing the plastic and the balloon gives them both the same charge, which makes them repel each other.

341. Spinning Matchsticks

Duration of Experiment: 15 mins.   Difficulty Level:

What you need:

2 copper coins   Matchsticks   Plastic cup   Balloon

What to do:

Step 1. Balance one coin vertically on the other.

Step 2. Balance the matchstick horizontally on this.

Step 3. Carefully put the plastic cup over this apparatus.

Step 4. Blow up the balloon and tie it.

Step 5. Rub the balloon against your hair and bring it near the glass.

Step 6. Watch as the matchstick follows the balloon.

> **What just happened?** Rubbing the balloon created a negative charge in the balloon. The matchstick has a neutral charge and was attracted to the balloon, which is why it 'followed' the balloon.

342. Making Lightning

Duration of Experiment: 10 mins.   Difficulty Level:

What you need:

Balloon   Sweater   Metal surface

What to do:

Step 1. Blow the balloon and go in a dark room.

Step 2. Rub the balloon vigorously against the sweater.

Step 3. Move the balloon close to the metal surface.

Step 4. There will be a spark between the balloon and the metal.

> **What just happened?** The balloon is being used to create static electricity. The flash or spark that jumps from the balloon to the metal object is like lightning, though much, much smaller in scale.

343. Balloon Attraction

Duration of Experiment: 🕐 10 mins.   Difficulty Level: ▬ ▬ ▬

What you need:

2 balloons

String

Woollen fabric

What to do:

Step 1. Blow up two balloons and tie strings to them.

Step 2. Hold the balloons from the strings about 3 cm apart. Notice that they are neutral.

Step 3. Rub one balloon against the woollen fabric.

Step 4. Watch as the balloons get attracted to each other.

Step 5. Now rub the other balloon to the woollen fabric as well.

Step 6. Notice how they repel each other.

💡 **What just happened?** Before rubbing the balloon, both had neutral charges and were neither attracted to nor repelled by each other. When you rubbed only one balloon, it got charged. The second balloon, however, was still neutral, so they were attracted to each other. However, when both balloons were rubbed, both of them got charged and repelled each other.

344. Illuminating Balloon

Duration of Experiment: 10 mins. Difficulty Level: ▬ ▬▬ ▬▬

What you need:

Bulb   Balloon

What to do:

Step 1. In a dark room, rub the balloon to your hair for five minutes.

Step 2. Touch it to the light bulb.

Step 3. You will be able to see sparks.

What just happened? When the charged balloon touched the bulb, electrons passed from the balloon to the bulb, causing it to emit small sparks of light.

345. Light It

Duration of Experiment: 10 mins. Difficulty Level: ▬ ▬▬ ▬▬

What you need:

Tubelight   Balloon

What to do:

Step 1. Blow the balloon.

Step 2. Go to a dark room.

Step 3. Rub the tube light with the balloon.

Step 4. Hold the balloon to the end of the tube light.

Step 5. It will light up.

What just happened? The ends of the tube light are sensitive to electric currents. As soon as it comes in contact with the balloon which you charged by rubbing, it lights up.

346. Balloony

Duration of Experiment: ⏱ 10 mins. Difficulty Level: ▬ ▬ ▬

What you need:

Styrofoam balls

Balloon

What to do:

Step 1. Fill the balloon with styrofoam balls.

Step 2. Inflate the balloon and tie it.

Step 3. Rub the balloon to your hair.

Step 4. Watch the balls in the balloon jump around!

💡 **What just happened?** As the static electricity jumped around in the balloon, the styrofoam balls too were attracted, then repelled by the walls of the balloon, causing them to jump around.

347. Static Ghost

Duration of Experiment: ⏱ 20 mins. Difficulty Level: ▬ ▬ ▬

What you need:

Books   Glycerine   Paintbrush   Glass pane   Tissue paper   Woollen fabric

What to do:

Step 1. Paint a face on the glass pane using glycerine.

Step 2. Place the glass, with the glycerine painted side facing down, an inch above with the help of the books.

Step 3. Finely shred the tissue. Put it under the glass.

Step 4. Rub the glass with the woollen fabric.

See your invisible face come into sight!

💡 **What just happened?** The static caused the paper to stick to the glass. The glycerine made sure it remained stuck.

CURRENT AFFAIRS
Experiments on the principle of electricity

Almost everything that we take for granted today runs on electricity. The TV, computer, phone, lights and fans—EVERYTHING works because of electricity.

Electricity is nothing but a constant flow of electrons. In this section, you will learn a lot about the elementary principles behind electricity.

Remember that electricity can be dangerous. Perform all these experiments only under adult supervision.

348. Conductor of Electricity

Duration of Experiment: ⏱ 10 mins.   Difficulty Level: ▭▬▬ ▬ ▬

What you need:

Battery   Flashlight bulb   Aluminium foil   Coin   Tape   Scissors   Clip

What to do:

Step 1. Cut the aluminium foil to make two 60 cm strips.

Step 2. Tape one end of both strips to the battery.

Wrap the other end around the base of the bulb.

Step 3. Use the clip to hold it in place.

Step 4. Now, touch the base of the bulb to the coin. See the bulb light up!

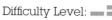

💡 **What just happened?** Some materials allow electricity to pass through them easily and some do not. The coin completes the circuit by allowing electricity to pass through it.

349. Simple Motor

Duration of Experiment: ⏱ **20** mins. Difficulty Level: ▬▬ ▬

What you need:

Battery   3 neodymium magnets   Copper wire

What to do:

Step 1. Remove the rubber covering from the wire.

Step 2. Twist the wire into a shape that can balance on the top of the battery as well as around the magnets.

Step 3. Arrange the objects as shown in the image.

Step 4. Watch the wire rotate.

💡 **What just happened?** Charge runs through the wire. The north and south poles of the magnet attract and repel the charge continuously, causing the wire to spin.

350. Coin Power

Duration of Experiment: ⏱ **15** mins. Difficulty Level: ▬▬ ▬

What you need:

Lemon   Tissue strips   Bowl   Coins – copper and stainless steel

What to do:

Step 1. Squeeze the lemon into the bowl. Dip the tissue strips in it.

Step 3. Make a tower of alternating copper and non-copper coins, separated by the lemon soaked strips, until your tower reaches a total of 10 coins.

Step 4. Wet your first finger and thumb. You will feel a mild shock!

💡 **What just happened?** The two types of coins have different electrical charges. The lemon acts as an acid and conducts this electricity. By stacking the coins on top of each other, the charge increased till it was enough to give you a shock.

351. Light it Up

Duration of Experiment: **30** mins.   Difficulty Level:

What you need:

| Tape | Light bulb | 3 wires | 1 battery (4.5 volt) | 1 paper clip | Cardboard | Thumbtack |

What to do:

Step 1. Remove half an inch of the insulation from each end of all three wires.

Step 2. Tape one end of one of the wires to the positive terminal of the battery. Tape the other end to a paper clip.

Step 3. Use a thumbtack to secure the end of that paper clip to the cardboard.

Step 4. Wrap one end of another wire to the side of the light bulb and the other end to the negative terminal of the battery.

Step 5. Wrap one end of the third wire around the negative terminal of the battery and place the other end near the paper clip.

Step 6. Touch the paper clip to the end of the third wire to see the bulb light up. You can now use the paper clip as a switch to turn the bulb on and off.

What just happened? All the materials used in the circuit are good conductors of electricity as they allow electrons to flow freely through them. This free flow of electrons provides energy, which lights up the bulb.

352. Dead or Alive?

Duration of Experiment: ⏱ 1 hour   Difficulty Level: ▬ ▬ ▬

What you need:

| Dead dry cell | Salt | Jar | Cloth | Flashlight | Water | Pin |

What to do:

Step 1. Make several holes in the top of the dead dry cell.

Step 2. Dissolve a packet of salt in the large jar of water.

Step 3. Place the cell in the jar.

Step 4. After an hour, take it out. Dry it with the cloth.

Step 5. Put it in a flashlight and watch the bulb light up.

💡 **What just happened?** When a battery dies, the liquid in the battery called 'electrolyte' dries up. Salt water is a substitute for the electrolyte. So when the battery soaks in the salt, it replaces the electrolyte and revives the battery.

353. Ice Tray Battery

Duration of Experiment: ⏱ 10 mins.   Difficulty Level: ▬ ▬ ▬

What you need:

| Distilled white vinegar | 5 pieces of copper wire | 5 galvanised nails | 1 Ice tray | 5mm 1 LED light |

What to do:

Step 1. Wrap all the nails with pieces of copper wire, leaving a section extending below the head of the nails.

Step 2. Fill six wells of an ice tray with distilled white vinegar.Insert each nail into a vinegar well, placing the wire in the next well.

Step 3. Place the "legs" of an LED light as shown. If it doesn't light, flip the legs.

💡 **What just happened?** Batteries comprise two different metals. When they are suspended in an acidic solution, the current flows out of the wire and into the nail.

354. Glowing Lead

Duration of Experiment: 10 mins.   Difficulty Level:

What you need:

Electric tape

Cardboard tube

Glass jar

Alligator clips

8 D-sized batteries

Aluminium plate

0.5 mm pencil lead

What to do:

Step 1. Tape the D-sized batteries together, with the positive end of one battery touching the negative end of the other.

Step 2. Cut the tube to a height that fits comfortably in the glass jar.

Step 3. Tape one positive and one negative alligator clip to one end of the tube.

Step 4. Carefully place a mechanical pencil lead between the two alligator clips.

Step 5. Place the glass jar over the top of the tube stand and the plate under it, as shown.

Step 6. Touch the other ends of the alligator clips to the ends of the battery.

Step 7. In a moment, the pencil lead begins to glow.

💡 **What just happened?** You completed the circuit by touching the ends of the alligator clips to the battery. This flow of electricity heats the pencil lead to an incredible temperature, which makes it glow and let out smoke.

355. Lighten Up!

Duration of Experiment: **20** mins.   Difficulty Level: ▬ ▬▬ ▬▬

What you need:

Battery   Flashlight bulb   5 inch wire   Tape   Paper cutter

What to do:

Step 1. Scrape the insulation off both ends of the wire.

Step 2. Curl one end of the wire tightly around the grooves at the base of the bulb.

Step 3. Shape the other end into a coil.

Step 4. Tape the coil to the bottom of a dry cell.

Step 5. Tape the rest of the wire to the cell such that the base of the bulb can touch the positive terminal of the battery.

SCIENCE AROUND US

How do electric switches work?

Switches work in a similar manner to the circuits you just made. When the switch is in an 'on' position, it completes the circuit. That is how electrons flow and whatever appliance you are switching 'on' works. On the other hand, in an 'off' position, the circuit is broken. This causes the flow of electrons to stop and the appliance to stop working.

What just happened? By connecting the positive and negative terminals of the battery, you completed the circuit, causing electricity to flow. This electric power lit up the bulb.

356. Magnetic Circuit

Duration of Experiment: ⏱ 10 mins. Difficulty Level: ▬ ▬ ▬

What you need:

4 ft copper wire   Compass   Bar magnet   Paper cutter

What to do:

Step 1. Scrape the insulation from both ends of the wire.

Step 2. Leave a foot on each end and coil the middle around four fingers.

Step 3. Join both ends of the wire.

Step 4. Move the magnet in and out of the coil.

Step 5. Hold the compass near the coil. The needle of the compass jiggles.

💡 **What just happened?** Placing a wire across a moving magnetic field causes a current to flow through the wire. Such a path is called a circuit.

357. Electric Telegraph

Duration of Experiment: ⏱ 10 mins. Difficulty Level: ▬ ▬ ▬

What you need:

3-volt light bulb   6-volt lantern battery   30 ft insulated wire

What to do:

Step 1. Build a long circuit by connecting the terminals of a bulb and the terminals of the battery cell with the wire.

Step 2. Keep the bulb and battery in different rooms.

Step 3. Disconnect one terminal of the battery and reconnect it. Send short or long bursts of light according to any code that you and your friends develop.

Step 4. You can now send a message to your friend in another room!

💡 **What just happened?** This is the concept that telegraphs were based on. Telegraphs were popular for a long time in the olden days.

358. The Mysterious Portrait

Duration of Experiment: 🕐 **10** mins.   Difficulty Level: ▬ ▬ ▬

What you need:

Pencil   Glue   Battery   Iron fillings   3 cardboard sheets   Wire   Scissors

What to do:

Step 1. Draw a face on one of the cardboards sheets. Cut it out.

Step 2. Paste this on another cardboard sheets.

Step 3. Stick the wire on the outline of the face.

Step 4. Paste the last cardboard sheets on top of this to conceal the face.

Step 5. Sprinkle iron fillings on the cardboard and connect the wire to the battery.

Step 6. Tap the cardboard and watch the fillings magically form a face.

💡 **What just happened?** By connecting the wire to a battery, the electric circuit was complete. This created a magnetic field around the wire, which means that the wire begins to act as a magnet. This attracts the iron fillings and they create a face.

ALL ELSE UNDER THE SUN
Miscellaneous Experiments

Though you may not believe it, science is present in everything around you. From the space stations in outer space to the fact that you are sitting here right now, reading this book – there is a scientific explanation for everything – well, almost everything.

This section is based on no theme in particular, but is a miscellaneous collection of experiments that did not fit into any other section.

359. Banana Tattoo

Duration of Experiment: 🕐 **30** mins.   Difficulty Level: ▬▬ ▬ ▬

What you need:

Banana   Toothpick   Paper   Pencil

What to do:

Step 1. Draw any tattoo shape on the paper.

Step 2. Place the paper on the banana and trace the shape with the toothpick. Make sure that the toothpick pierces the banana skin.

Step 3. Wait for half an hour.

You now have a tattooed banana!

💡 **What just happened?** When the peel of the banana is cut or bruised, an enzyme called 'polyphenol oxidase' is released. This reacts with air, causing the brown colour.

360. Balloon Kebab

Duration of Experiment: ⏱ 15 mins.   Difficulty Level: ▬ ▬ ▬

What you need:

Skewer   Petroleum jelly   Balloons

What to do:

Step 1. Blow up the balloon and tie it.

Step 2. Spread the petroleum jelly all over the skewer.

Step 3. Insert the skewer with a gentle twisting motion into the balloon from next to the knot.

Step 4. Once the skewer emerges from the opposite end, you have your balloon kebab!

Step 5. If you try to skewer the balloon horizontally, it won't be as easy.

SCIENCE AROUND US

What are polymers?

Polymers are long chains of hundreds or thousands of tiny molecules. Rubber is a polymer. Under tension, these links can stretch, which allows rubber to expand. However, the links eventually break under too much pressure, which is how a balloon bursts!

💡 **What just happened?** The balloon is less stretched out near the knot and opposite than the middle. This allows the tip of the skewer to push aside the molecules of rubber, and slide into the balloon. However, enough cross-links remain so that the balloon holds together.

361. Glowing Flower

Duration of Experiment: ⏱ 3 hours   Difficulty Level: ▬▬ ▬▬ ▬▬

What you need:

Highlighter pen   Water   Flower   Scissors   UV light

What to do:

Step 1. Open the highlighter and squeeze the dye from the ink pad into a little water.

Step 2. Cut half the stem of the flower and place it in the inky water.

Step 3. Look at it under the UV light after 2 hours, preferably in a dark room.

💡 **What just happened?** The water gets sucked all the way up to the petals through capillary action. This makes the flower glow under the UV light.

362. Funny Reflections

Duration of Experiment: ⏱ 3-5 mins.   Difficulty Level: ▬▬ ▬▬ ▬▬

What you need:

Spoon

What to do:

Step 1. Look at your face on both sides of the spoon.

Step 2. Don't you look funny?

💡 **What just happened?** The spoon is like a mirror, but with a curve in it. The front is called a 'concave' surface and the back is called a 'convex' surface. Light is reflected in a straight line in a mirror. From both, convex and concave surfaces, light is bent as it reflects back. That's what makes the reflections funny.

363. Bubble Painting

Duration of Experiment: ⏱ 15 mins.   Difficulty Level: ▬ ▬

What you need:

Straw   Dishwashing   Watercolour   Paper   Cups   Water
           liquid   paint

What to do:

Step 1. Add two tablespoons of coloured paint, one tablespoon
of water and two tablespoons of dishwashing liquid in a cup.

Step 2. Use the straw to blow into the mixture till the cup overflows.

Step 3. Lay the paper on top of the bubbles and observe the prints.

Step 4. Let it dry and repeat with another colour.

💡 **What just happened?** Though we can't see the colour in the bubble since its
wall is only a few millimetres thick, the bubble carries these colours to the paper
and deposits them there, creating beautiful prints.

364. Look at Sunspots

Duration of Experiment: ⏱ 30 mins.   Difficulty Level: ▬ ▬

What you need:

Pin   Butter paper   Shoe box   Tape

What to do:

Step 1. Make a pin-hole on one side of the shoe box.

Step 2. Cut out the other side and cover it with butter paper.

Step 3. Seal the shoe box shut and point the hole towards the Sun
such that the image of the Sun falls on the opposite side of the shoe box.

Step 4. Observe the butter paper to see if you can see dark spots of the bright image of
the Sun. You may have to repeat the experiment on several days to see the spots.

💡 **What just happened?** The Sun is not uniformly of the same temperature. Some
spots on the Sun are cooler than the rest of the Sun. These spots are called 'sunspots'.

365. Recycled Paper

Duration of Experiment: 24 hours Difficulty Level:

What you need:

Rolling pin   Sieve   Newspaper   Blender   Water   Cloth   2 planks of wood

What to do:

Step 1. Put the newspaper in the blender. Add water and blend it till it is a nice, smooth paste.

Step 2. Pour this paste through the sieve to drain out the water.

Step 3. Put the pulp onto the cloth and flatten it with a rolling pin.

Step 4. Cover the top of the paper with another cloth.

Step 5. Put the cloth with the paper between two planks of wood.

Step 6. Stand on it to flatten it out.

Step 7. Let it dry overnight. You can now enjoy your recycled paper.

SCIENCE AROUND US

How is paper recycled on a large scale?

The basic process behind recycling is the same in the large plants as your homemade paper. The only difference is in the machines used. Huge mixers are used to create the slurry and huge rollers are then used to flatten them out.

What just happened? Paper is made up of long fibres from wood or vegetable products. While recycling paper, you separated these fibres and rearranged them. Every time you recycle paper the fibres get shorter, which limits the number of times the same paper can be recycled.

ISBN: 978-81-87107-58-3

ISBN: 978-81-87107-57-6

ISBN: 978-81-87107-56-9

ISBN: 978-81-87107-53-8

ISBN: 978-93-84225-31-5

ISBN: 978-93-81607-49-7

ISBN: 978-81-87107-55-2

ISBN: 978-81-87107-52-1

ISBN: 978-93-84225-32-2

ISBN: 978-93-80070-84-1

ISBN: 978-93-80070-83-4

ISBN: 978-93-80069-36-4

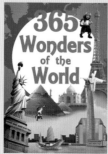

ISBN: 978-93-80069-35-7

ISBN: 978-93-80070-79-7

ISBN: 978-93-84625-92-4

ISBN: 978-93-84225-33-9

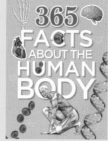

ISBN: 978-93-84625-93-1

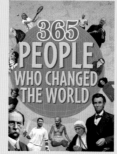

ISBN: 978-93-84225-34-6

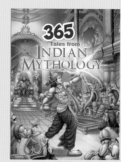

ISBN: 978-81-87107-46-0